D0356558

Why Can't My Son Read?

Success Strategies for Helping Boys With Dyslexia and Reading Difficulties

Why Can't My Son Read?

Ellen Burns Hurst, Ph.D.,
& Michael Richard Hurst, J.D.

PRUFROCK PRESS INC.
WACO, TEXAS

CALGARY PUBLIC LIBRARY

OCT 2014

Acknowledgements

We would like to acknowledge all the boys who struggle with dyslexia and any reading difficulty. The faces of all the boys with whom we have worked streamed before our eyes as each page was written. The pain and courage of each parent whom we have had the privilege to support is etched on our hearts. This book is written for them and all the boys whose lives we can't touch. We hope our words in some way ease their pain and that of their parents.

Many thanks and appreciation is also given to our children. Zac Hurst, Michelle Hurst, Liz Ruth, and Brent Ruth have provided constant love and encouragement to us in this venture. Our oldest son, Dr. Eric Hurst, continues to provide unique support as our mentor. To have a child as a mentor is a unique and wonderful experience. Our first grandchild, Aiden Zachary Hurst, was born on February 16, 2014, and will face the challenge of learning to read in a hostile world. May God and all his angels protect Aiden on his journey.

Library of Congress catalog information
currently on file with the publisher.

Copyright ©2015, Prufrock Press Inc.

Edited by Bethany Johnsen

Cover and layout design by Raquel Trevino

ISBN-13: 978-1-61821-238-2

No part of this book may be reproduced, translated, stored in a retrieval system, or transmitted, in any form or by any means, electronic, mechanical, photocopying, microfilming, recording, or otherwise, without written permission from the publisher.

Printed in the United States of America.

At the time of this book's publication, all facts and figures cited are the most current available. All telephone numbers, addresses, and websites URLs are accurate and active. All publications, organizations, websites, and other resources exist as described in the book, and all have been verified. The author and Prufrock Press Inc. make no warranty or guarantee concerning the information and materials given out by organizations or content found at websites, and we are not responsible for any changes that occur after this book's publication. If you find an error, please contact Prufrock Press Inc.

Prufrock Press Inc.
P.O. Box 8813
Waco, TX 76714-8813
Phone: (800) 998-2208
Fax: (800) 240-0333
http://www.prufrock.com

Table of Contents

CHAPTER 1

A Recipe for Failure

"Something is rotten in the state of boys' education, and I can't help but think that the pattern I have seen in my classroom may have something to do with a collective failure to adequately educate boys." These words were written by Jessica Lahey (2013), but anyone who looks at the grim statistics on boys in school might be tempted to agree. Boys get expelled from preschool at nearly five times the rate of girls—and that's only the beginning. Compared to girls, boys are twice as likely to be held back a grade, four times more likely to be diagnosed with learning disabilities and attention problems, account for 70% of D's and F's, are 30% more likely to drop out of school, and make up only 43% of college students (Gurian & Stevens, 2004; Reichert & Hawley, 2010).

Educators share a duty to create an America with equitable learning opportunities for every student in the classroom. The focus on providing appropriate opportunities for boys is a relatively recent issue, but one that school systems are addressing with increasing urgency. A study on gender disparities in elementary school performance examined both the objective and subjective aspects of boys' deteriorating academic performance (Cornwell, Mustard, & Van Parys, 2013). Surprisingly, it showed that the grades awarded by teachers are not aligned with test scores. Girls in every racial category outperform boys on reading tests, while boys score at least as well on math and science tests as girls. However, boys in all racial categories across all subject areas are not represented in grade distributions where their test scores would predict.

There are some exceptions to this puzzling phenomenon. Boys who shared the girls' positive attitude toward learning received the same grade. The well-socialized boys received a higher grade for good behavior. In short, boys who match girls on both test scores and behavior get better grades than girls, while boys who match girls on test scores but have bad behavior are graded more harshly. This means that the issue of what to do with underperforming boys just became much more complicated (Christakis, 2013).

Identifying the Issues

The U.S. Department of Education reading tests for the last 30 years show boys scoring worse than girls in every age group, every year. The following are a few possible explanations for why boys are having reading trouble:

- ➤ Biologically, boys are slower to develop than girls and often struggle with reading and writing skills early on.
- ➤ The action-oriented, competitive learning style of many boys works against them learning to read and write.
- ➤ Many books boys are asked to read don't appeal to them. They aren't motivated to read.
- ➤ Our society teaches boys to suppress feelings. Many boys don't feel comfortable exploring the emotions found in fiction.
- ➤ Boys don't have enough positive male role models for literacy. Because the majority of adults involved in kids' reading are women, boys might not see reading as a masculine activity.

The frightening fact is that as boys get older, they increasingly describe themselves as nonreaders. This perception of self as a nonreader could manifest itself as avoidance of reading because of below-grade-level skills, feelings of defeat that turn off the desire to read, or sidestepping situations that have the potential to expose him to the shame related to poor oral reading skills. Few boys have this attitude early in their schooling, but nearly 50% describe themselves as non-readers by the time they enter secondary school (Beers, 1996).

The downward spiral continues as boys in middle and high school report fewer social supports, less self-efficacy, and lower intrinsic motivation than girls of the same age. In particular, boys admit to putting significantly less effort into their schoolwork and preparing for class than girls describe (Madden & Allen, 2006).

Where does this discrepancy begin? Answering this question requires that we take a long, hard look at what is happening in early childhood education. Boys start off their schooling on the wrong foot when they enter kindergarten classrooms that are mismatched with their phase of development and intolerant of their unique style of play.

Inappropriate Academic Expectations

Ask a kindergarten teacher the following question: How long can the average 5-year-old boy sit still, be quiet, and pay attention—compared with the average 5-year-old girl? Most teachers will tell you that the boy cannot sit still, be quiet, and pay attention for nearly as long as the girl. The boy starts squirming, fidgeting, and getting restless. Behavior and abilities that are developmentally appropriate for a 5-year-old girl may not be developmentally appropriate for a 5-year-old boy.

The most profound difference between girls and boys is not in any brain structure per se, but rather in the developmental sequence of the various brain regions. The fact that different brain regions develop in a different order, and at a different rate, for boys versus girls is a key insight from the past 5 years of neuroscientific research on brain development. The world's largest study of brain development in children (National Institutes of Health [NIH], 2007) has demonstrated dramatic differences in the trajectories of brain development between genders.

There are significant differences in the development of language skills between boys and girls (Zull, 2004). Girls develop language skills sooner than boys. Girls consistently score higher on tests of verbal ability, read earlier, speak in more complex sentences, and understand abstract ideas faster. The use of sophisticated medical imaging devices is providing hard data to document differences in brain development and activity. This takes us from subjective anecdotal indicators of gender differences in children's language development to scientific fact. We now know that girls experience the cognitive changes that affect language acquisition at age 14–20 months. Boys reveal these transformations later, at 20–24 months of age. This can clarify why girls often speak sooner than boys, use larger vocabularies, and speak in multiple-word sentences or phrases.

Advantages for girls continue along the developmental process. The prefrontal cortex—the part of the brain that controls expression, verbal skill, and cognitive and social behavior—in adolescent girls not only develops earlier but is larger than that of adolescent boys (Zull, 2004). Adolescent girls' neural connectors expedite communication between the right and left brains. This means better focus, better listening skills, better memory, and better multitasking—in short, more areas of the brain devoted to the skills required for reading, writing, and verbal fluency.

Today's American classrooms are set up in favor of girls' faster brain development. In my kindergarten classroom, you would have seen kids doing lots of different things: singing, dancing, playing, finger painting, and maybe even a little formal instruction. Walk into almost any kindergarten today, and you will see something quite different. The kindergarten of today looks very much like first grade did 30 years ago. Proponents of an academic kindergarten would point out that we must be at the forefront of our global economy. Ironically, some of those countries that outscore us on international assessments start children in school later than we do.

Sax (2013) asserted that it is not difficult to explain why starting kids in school 2 years later produces superior performance. Academically oriented kindergarten programs force little boys to spend inordinate amounts of time on tasks they're just not ready to perform. For many boys, there's a huge difference in readiness to learn between age 5 and age 7. Most 5-year-old girls are better able to adapt to the rigorous academic character of kindergarten, but a 5-year-old boy would be at the same level of development as a 3-year-old girl (Sax, 2013).

Many parents understand that kindergarten is not a good match for their 5-year-old son. It has become common in affluent districts for parents to wait a year before they enroll their son, putting many boys in kindergarten classrooms at age 6 rather than age 5. This practice is called *redshirting*. However, in low-income neighborhoods, it is rare that boys will be redshirted. Low-income families are more likely to indicate concerns about their child's school readiness, but these families rarely delay kindergarten entry. The decision to delay kindergarten means finding and paying for another year of childcare, which is far too expensive for most low-income families (Bassok & Reardon, 2013). What a heartbreaking decision for a family to have to make.

Intolerance of Boys' Play

The following excerpts are from just two of the myriad articles describing recent overreactions to boys' behavior from school administrators.

> WACO, Texas—School administrators gave a 4-year-old student an in-school suspension for inappropriately touching a teacher's aide after the prekindergartner hugged the woman. A letter from La Vega school district administrators to the student's parents said that the boy was involved in "inappropriate physical behavior interpreted as sexual contact and/or sexual harassment" after he hugged the woman and he rubbed his face in the chest of the female employee on Nov. 10. DaMarcus Blackwell, the father of the boy who attends La Vega Primary School, said he filed a complaint with the district. He said that his son doesn't understand why he was punished. La Vega school district officials said student privacy laws pre-

vented them from commenting. After Blackwell filed a complaint, a subsequent letter from the district said the offense had been changed to inappropriate physical contact and removed references of sexual contact or sexual harassment from the boy's file. Administrators said the district's student handbook contains no specific guidelines referring to contact between teachers and students but does state that inappropriate physical contact will result in a discipline referral. ("Texas Child Suspended After Hugging Aide," 2006)

Child suspended from his Virginia school for picking up a pencil and using it to "shoot" a "bad guy"—his friend, who was also suspended. A few months earlier, Josh Welch, also 7, was sent home from his Maryland school for nibbling off the corners of a strawberry Pop-Tart to shape it into a gun. At about the same time, Colorado's Alex Evans, age 7, was suspended for throwing an imaginary hand grenade at "bad guys" in order to "save the world." (Sommers, 2013, p. 1)

Believe it or not, in each of the cases discussed by Sommers, school officials found the boys to be in violation of the school's zero-tolerance policies for firearms. In the name of zero tolerance, our schools are becoming hostile environments for young boys. Girls have fallen victim to these absurdities, but it is mostly boys who are targeted.

Across the country, schools are demonizing the assertive sociability of boys. Young boys love action narratives involving heroes, bad guys, rescues, and shoot-ups. As boys' play proceeds, imaginations soar and plots become more elaborate. Adam Gidwitz, author of the best-selling *A Tale Dark and Grimm* books, credits his success as an author to the time he spent in imaginative play as a child, inventing stories about his G.I. Joes (Gidwitz, 2010). During play, boys naturally learn the component parts of stories and novels while developing the skills of visualization and problem solving.

How can we find balance between imaginative play and play that escalates into real aggression? Logue and Harvey (2010) reported that play escalates into real aggression about one percent of the time. Yet, as they surveyed classroom practices of 98 teachers of 4-year-olds, they found that boys' action narrative was the play format least tolerated. Nearly half of teachers stopped or redirected boys' dramatic play daily or several times a week.

Imaginative play is a critical basis for learning. Logue and Harvey (2010) found that action narratives improve children's conversation and imaginative writing. In addition, unstructured play also builds moral imagination and social competence and imparts critical lessons about personal limits and self-restraint. When we focus on the literacy gap experienced by boys, it seems possible that the intolerance for boys' action-narrative play choices may be undermining their early language development and weakening their attachment to school.

The Path to Success

Now that you have a solid understanding of the common obstacles to boys' success in school, how can you tear them down? As a parent, you may not be able to singlehandedly correct the structural disadvantages to boys in the American education system, but you *can* make sure your son doesn't fall victim to them. The following chapters impart the information that you will need to know to help your son become a better reader.

In Chapter 2, Complex Diagnosis, we attempt to distinguish the distinct but related phenomena of not being *able* to read and not being *willing* to read. Understanding the root causes of some boys' difficulty processing text and lack of motivation to do so is the first step to solving these problems. Then, Chapters 3 and 4 will address boys' disinclination to read, and Chapters 5 and 6 will address dyslexia.

Chapter 3, Attention and Executive Function, provides important information on working with boys with high energy levels or those who may have ADHD. The ability to focus is, of course, a necessary prerequisite for reading, and this chapter will help you get your son there.

Chapter 4, Competition and Motivation, introduces the idea that there are both helpful and detrimental forms of competition (rather than labelling all competition as "good" or "bad" for kids), and discusses specific types of competition that may motivate your son to work on his reading.

Chapter 5, Mistaught, discusses how reading instruction is frequently mishandled in the school system, much to the detriment of children who process text differently. Some professionals from whom you seek help for your struggling son may not have the skills or knowledge to provide it. Faced with this realization, you must arm yourself with the information needed to both teach and advocate for your son.

Chapter 6, What Parents Can Do at Home to Increase Reading Abilities, equips you with practical tools and strategies to provide the effective reading instruction at home that your son may not be obtaining at school. Here you will find the nuts and bolts of reading intervention for all aspects of the reading process. In addition, suggestions for the use of technology to improve reading skills are provided.

The last chapter is your guide to advocacy. We hope that you are in a situation in which you are working as a partner with your son's school to improve his performance. If that is not the case, Chapter 7, Becoming Your Son's Advocate, will give you an overview of your legal rights as well as links to more in-depth legal expertise. We hope you will feel inspired and informed.

Appendix A: Books Boys Love is a list of titles that may interest your son. You can also learn about books that appeal to boys online; check out initiatives such as Guys Read (http://www.guysread.com), which offer helpful resources to inspire the reluctant male reader. Our own list was mostly compiled from boys' answers to a *Creative Kids* magazine informal survey of favorite books, in conjunction with the information (also largely derived from informal surveys) provided by Guys Read and similar initiatives. The best way to find out what boys like to read is to ask.

Appendix B: Glossary of Reading Terms is your easy reference for navigating the jargon of the reading instruction field. Whether you encounter terms you aren't familiar with when speaking to educators, in formal or informal reports regarding your son, or within the pages of this book, just flip to Appendix B to quickly get up to speed.

CHAPTER 2

Complex Diagnosis
Can't Read or Won't Read?

Ellen was a high school teacher for 20 years. For 18 of those years, her job was to coordinate a program for students who had been identified as potential dropouts. The criteria to be accepted into the program were simple: If a student was in ninth grade and had already reach the age of 16 (the legal drop out age in Georgia), scored below the 25th percentile on a standardized reading test, received free or reduced lunch, was homeless, or spoke a first language other than English, the student qualified.

When Ellen first accepted this position, she was young and naïvely undaunted by the task of keeping these adolescents in school. But the intense everyday challenges of the job soon shook her faith in her ability to put her students on the right track. She almost didn't return to school after a bright 18-year-old who was 6 weeks from graduation dropped out. When asked why, he gave a disheartening explanation: His family had told him that if he graduated from high school, he would be too good for them. He would have been the first in all generations to graduate—but he couldn't bear the rejection of his family.

9

Ellen experienced so many stories of school failure. Mostly boys. Most came from homes that needed them to work and add financial support to the family or babysit their younger siblings. They had no peer group with whom to eat lunch, so they would stand around the walls of the cafeteria not eating, even though they qualified for free lunch. It was too humiliating to go through the line and show the card that marked them as poor. Some never went to the bathroom all day because of the teasing they would get from the popular crowd or gang members. Many smelled because they lived in homes with no running water and therefore no showers. Most hated reading because they never received the interventions they needed to improve. They equated reading with shame. Most hated school—can you blame them? For these boys, as for most Ellen has worked with, not being *able* to read and not being *willing* to read were intimately related. Regardless of which comes first for a particular student, difficulty with reading or lack of motivation to read, one generally leads to the other. It's a self-perpetuating cycle that must be stopped and replaced with a positive learner identity for your son.

School is a social context that provides the social dynamics of the world within which students learn and construct their learner identities (Lave & Wenger, 1998). Boys who don't read are branded with culturally imposed identities. This branding results in denied entry into elite groups.

Identity labels can be used to stereotype, privilege, or marginalize readers and writers as "struggling "or "proficient," as "creative" or "deviant" (Lin, 2008). Pressley (2002) emphasized that students in the intermediate grades who still struggle with word recognition read less because reading becomes unrewarding; thus practice reading is avoided, precluding eventual growth and development. Stanovich (2000) described this phenomenon as a "downward spiral" for students, suggesting that if word-level difficulties are not overcome, the students' experiences with reading become worse. The institutions in which one learns to read rely heavily on identities that take the form of progress indicators. These identity labels can be especially powerful in an individual's life. What and how one reads and writes can have an impact on the type of person one is recognized as being and on how one sees oneself. Words, texts, and the literate practices that accompany them not only reflect but may also produce the self (Davies, 2003).

Because of the importance of being both able and willing to read in today's society, we will examine these related but distinct issues separately.

Boys Who Won't Read

Since the beginning of the National Assessment of Education Progress in the late 1960s, there has been a gender gap in reading, which is measured at ages 9, 13, and 17. The gap is largest just as boys are considering what to do after graduation, taking the SATs and ACTs—11 points (National Center for Education Statistics [NCES], 2014).

The decision not to go to college does not alleviate the necessity of having strong literacy skills. It is not only college courses but the job market that demand high-level reading and writing skills (Tyre, 2008). If you lacked reading skills 40 years ago, there were still plenty of employment opportunities. Today, many jobs for unskilled workers have been outsourced overseas. There are no illiterate scientists, auto mechanics, and engineers. Boys have been losing ground in the very skills we know are now essential.

Although today's boys have a multitude of new media attractions to lure them away from books, boys' lack of enthusiasm for reading is not a recent phenomenon. Peg Tyre (2008) said that the issue has existed for centuries. She pointed out that John Locke lamented in the 18th century that male students were not able to write as well as female students, and he marveled at how much more easily girls picked up foreign languages.

Gender is a significant factor at play in determining performance in reading and writing, but it is not the only factor. We cannot lose sight of the fact that the differences among boys and among girls are greater than the differences between boys and girls. We must be careful not to focus on the gender differences between students, but rather to recognize that the effectiveness of certain approaches in literacy instruction may be tied to gender. If we keep this focus, we will be better able to provide appropriate and equitable opportunities for both boys and girls. There are four distinct categories of students who don't read:

➤ The dormant reader: "I'm too busy right now!"
➤ The uncommitted reader: "I might be a reader, someday."
➤ The unmotivated reader: "I'm never going to like it!"
➤ The disabled reader: "It doesn't make sense."

By understanding these views, we can gain greater insight into why some boys choose not to read. Researchers have identified many generalized gender differences related to literacy that teachers encounter in their work with individual learners. With respect to achievement, (Smith & Wilhelm, 2002):

➤ Boys take longer to learn to read than girls do.
➤ Boys read less than girls.
➤ Girls tend to comprehend narrative texts and most expository texts significantly better than boys do.
➤ Boys tend to be better at information retrieval and work-related literacy tasks than girls are.

With respect to attitude (Smith & Wilhelm, 2002):

➤ Boys generally provide lower estimations of their reading abilities than girls do.
➤ Boys value reading as an activity less than girls do.
➤ Boys have much less interest in pleasure reading than girls do, and are far more likely to read for utilitarian purposes than girls are.
➤ Significantly more boys than girls declare themselves to be nonreaders.
➤ Boys express less enthusiasm for reading than girls do.

With respect to text choice, boys like to read (Moloney, 2002):

➤ books that reflect their image of themselves—what they aspire to be and to do;

> books that make them laugh and that appeal to their sense of mischief;
> fiction that focuses on action more than on emotions;
> books in series, such as the Harry Potter series, which seem to provide boys with a sense of comfort and familiarity;
> science fiction or fantasy;
> newspapers, magazines, and informational nonfiction;
> comic books, baseball cards, and instruction manuals; and
> materials that are often not available in the classroom.

Interestingly, when they read these materials, many boys do not consider themselves to be reading at all, precisely because these materials are not valued at school (Moloney, 2002).

Smith and Wilhelm (2002) suggested providing boys with texts that:

> are "storied," using a narrative approach that focuses more on plot and action than on description;
> are visual (e.g., graphic novels), providing a multimedia experience;
> are musical, providing the opportunity to develop literacy skills through an exploration of lyrics and discussions about musical tastes, and the role of music in students' lives;
> provide "exportable knowledge"—that is, information boys can use in conversation;
> sustain engagement, such as books in series or collections that allow readers to follow characters they have come to care about;
> show multiple perspectives, exploring topics from a variety of points of view;
> are novel or unexpected in a school setting, such as satire;
> are edgy or controversial—worth arguing and caring about;
> contain powerful or positive ideas that have political, moral, or "life-expanding" appeal;
> are funny, appealing to boys' taste for humor. (pp. 150–157)

Books with one or more of these characteristics can be found in Appendix A: Books Boys Love. An exhaustive list of books your son could potentially enjoy would be infinite, of course, but we have tried to provide enough titles to get a parent started.

Many parents have certain fixed ideas about what their children "should" be reading. These ideas of what constitutes quality literature often exclude books that appeal especially to boys (e.g., graphic novels, books that contain "potty humor"). It is true that some texts are of higher literary quality than others, and wanting to see your son develop a taste for such material is natural. It is also fair to argue that some of boys' reading preferences (e.g., books that don't focus on emotions, books about other boys) are the product of the negative cultural influences on young men that reading ought to counteract. Perhaps, rather than just going along with the tired idea that "girls will read books about boys, but boys won't read books about girls," we ought to be encouraging our sons to take interest in the lives of women and other people who are unlike them. All of these ideas are very valid. However, as a parent, it is important for you to set aside any considerations that prompt you to discourage your son from reading what he likes or to redirect him to books that do not interest him. In the wise words of author Neil Gaiman (Brown, 2013):

> Well-meaning adults can easily destroy a child's love of reading. Stop them reading what they enjoy or give them worthy-but-dull books that you like—the 21st-century equivalents of Victorian 'improving' literature—you'll wind up with a generation convinced that reading is uncool and, worse, unpleasant. (para. 5)

Motivating a struggling or reluctant reader is difficult; do not make it impossible by forcing him to read books he sees as "uncool." A child can never derive any benefits from quality literature if he does not first discover that reading can be pleasurable. Get him to like reading, and who knows what wonderful literature he will eventually be exposed to. *Captain Underpants and the Perilous Plot of Professor Poopypants* is not the problem. Not reading is the problem.

Boys Who Can't Read

Estimates of the prevalence of reading disabilities vary widely, ranging from 4%–20% of school-aged children (Shaywitz et al., 1999). According to these figures, up to 10 million children in the United States have some form of reading disability.

Reading disabilities are diagnosed up to five times more frequently in boys than girls, although some sources claim that this figure is misleading because boys are more likely to be screened for learning disabilities due to their higher incidence of disruptive behavior, which draws the attention of educators and other professionals.

Definition of dyslexia. Sally Shaywitz (2003) defined developmental dyslexia as being characterized by an unexpected difficulty in reading experienced by children and adults who otherwise possess the intelligence and motivation considered sufficient for accurate and fluent reading. Dyslexia is the most common and most carefully studied of the learning disabilities, affecting 80% of all individuals identified as learning disabled.

For the purposes of clarity, the term *dyslexia* will be used in this book as a broad classification that encompasses all types of reading difficulties.

Causes of Dyslexia

A variety of causes have been advanced for developmental reading disorders. Researchers favoring a biological explanation have cited heredity, minimal brain dysfunction, delays in neurological development, and failure of the right and left hemispheres to function properly together. Critics of the neurological explanation of dyslexia still assert that it is nothing more than a plausible explanation of why children of privilege and intelligence could not learn to read as expected or a means of securing more time for labeled children on examinations (McDermott, Goldman, & Varenne, 2006). A reading disorder is often identified in kindergarten, when reading instruction begins. Yet even at the preschool stage, there may be indicators that foreshadow a reading disability. The International Dyslexia Association (IDA, 2014) suggested that the following are early indicators of dyslexia:

- ➤ delayed speech;
- ➤ mixing up the sounds and syllables in long words;
- ➤ chronic ear infections;
- ➤ severe reactions to childhood illnesses;
- ➤ constant confusion of left versus right;
- ➤ late establishing a dominant hand;
- ➤ difficulty learning to tie shoes;
- ➤ trouble memorizing their address, phone number, or the alphabet;
- ➤ inability to generate words that rhyme; and
- ➤ a close relative with dyslexia. (para. 3)

Many of the world's children suffer from dyslexia, yet very little is known about its causes. New research methods are beginning to shed light on the perplexing question of why boys with adequate schooling and at least average intelligence still have difficulties in reading, understanding, and explaining individual words or entire texts.

IDA resolved one aspect of the confusion by establishing a broad-based definition of dyslexia. IDA (2014) defined dyslexia as follows:

> Dyslexia is a specific learning disability that is neuro-logical in origin. It is characterized by difficulties with accurate and/or fluent word recognition and by poor spelling and decoding abilities. These difficulties typi-cally result from a deficit in the phonological compo-nent of language that is often unexpected in relation to other cognitive abilities and the provision of effec-tive classroom instruction. Secondary consequences may include problems in reading comprehension and reduced reading experience that can impede growth of vocabulary and background knowledge. (para. 1).

The IDA definition is vague relative to the issue of the neuro-logical origins of dyslexia. The definition minimizes the possibility that gender, race, class, and instructional practices could contribute to or exacerbate the propensity for developing this condition. Frith (1999) stated that in order to fully understand dyslexia, we need to link together cultural, biological, and behavioral factors. She claimed that we must consider the possibility that these each of these three factors, alone or in concert, can aggravate or ameliorate the condition.

Shaywitz (2003) enriched the definition of dyslexia based on the first neuroimaging studies of dyslexics. Technological advances in the form of functional MRIs substantiated the view that dyslexia is a neurodevelopmental disorder with a biological origin. There is also evidence to support the theory of a genetic component as a causative factor. Studies seek to isolate a specific causal gene (Nöthen et al., 1999). Knowledge of a genetic link could allow for earlier diagnoses and hopefully more successful interventions. Today, too many students are not diagnosed until high school, at which point treatments become more complex (Eicher & Gruen, 2013).

Eicher and Gruen (2013) analyzed data from more than 10,000 children born in 1991–1992 who were part of the Avon Longitudinal Study of Parents and Children (ALSPAC) conducted by investigators at the University of Bristol in the United Kingdom. They identified genetic variants that can predispose children to dyslexia and language impairment, increasing the likelihood of earlier diagnosis and more effective interventions.

Eicher and Gruen (2013) stated that these findings will help identify the pathways for fluent reading, the components of those pathways, and how they interact. It is their hope to be able to offer a pre-symptomatic diagnostic panel for early identification of children, thus increasing their chances of reading at grade level by providing early intervention.

Types of Dyslexia

The Dyslexia Institutes of America (DIA, 2014) described three distinct types of dyslexia.

Dyseidetic dyslexia. This type of dyslexia is associated with differential brain functions located in the angular gyrus of the left parietal lobe of the brain. People suffering from this type of dyslexia will have poor sight-word recognition, contributing to an overall slow and laborious reading experience. They tend to both sound out (laugh = log) and spell (ready = rede) irregular words phonetically (DIA, 2014).

Dysphonetic dyslexia. This type of dyslexia is associated with differential brain functions located in Wernicke's area of the left temporal and parietal lobes of the brain. A person suffering from this type of dyslexia relies on sight recognition to read, being unable to sound out unknown words; either skips unknown words or substitutes known words; and learns words by rote memorization, lacking the ability to spell them out by their sound (DIA, 2014).

Dysphoneidetic dyslexia. This type of dyslexia is associated with a combination of differential brain functions in the angular gyrus and Wernicke's area. A person suffering from this type of dyslexia will have weak visual-motor skills. This type is often the most difficult to treat (DIA, 2014).

Misconceptions About Dyslexia

The difficulties and concerns of a parent advocating for child with a reading disability are already significant. The confusion and popular misconceptions surrounding the diagnosis and treatment of dyslexia only add to the parental dilemma. In order to delve into the biological origins of dyslexia, it is imperative that these misconceptions be replaced with accurate facts. The following facts may surprise you.

1. Dyslexics do not write backward. The most common misconception concerning dyslexia is that it can be diagnosed when a student writes letters or words backward (Shaywitz, 2003). Teachers and parents become overly concerned when they see evidence of these reversals in the writing samples of children. Badian (2005) reported that reversal errors are likely to disappear in children with reading disabilities as their reading and writing skills improve. The observation of reversals is not unique to the reading and writing of struggling readers. During the developmental process of acquiring literacy, most children engage in some level of word and letter reversals before the age of 8. Shaywitz (2003) asserted that there is no evidence that dyslexics actually see letters and words backward. The core of dyslexia is not visual perception. The basis of dyslexia is a problem with processing language at the phoneme level. Phonemes are the representation of sounds that are meaningful within a language. These sounds allow individuals to distinguish one word from another. Thus, the deficiency in the person with dyslexia is the inability to distinguish the phonemic difference between "big" and "pig" rather than the ability to distinguish the graphic differences of the letters. Shaywitz (2003) expressed concern that many children will not be correctly diagnosed because they do not make the stereotypical reversals.

2. Dyslexia is not the result of a visual processing deficit. The assumption that dyslexia is the result of a visual processing deficit leads to a second common misconception. The use of colored text overlays or lenses is purported to be the quick fix for reading disabilities. Stone and Harris (1991) reviewed evidence for the existence of scotopic sensitivity syndrome (SSS). SSS allegedly is manifested as a visual disturbance related to light. Treatment for SSS includes the wearing of colored glasses or the use of colored plastic sheet overlays. Stone and Harris found that the diagnosis of this condition is extremely subjective and raises questions of accuracy and reliability of previous studies. A visual deficit in dyslexics is not the cause of the reading disability (Olulade, Napoliello, & Eden, 2013). There is a strong correlation between people's reading ability and brain activity in the visual system, but that does not mean that training the visual system will result in better reading.

3. Dyslexia does not affect more boys than girls. Gaub and Carlson (1997) suggested that the girls who are referred to clinics are those most severely affected. They trigger the referral process as a result of the "squeaking wheel" phenomenon by displaying co-occurring overt behavioral patterns of inattention. Szatmari's (1992) population studies found a ratio of identification of one girl for every three male diagnoses. Shaywitz (2003) gave evidence that as many girls are affected by dyslexia as are boys. She suggested that the reason that the overidentification of boys occurs is the manifestation of gender specific behavior. The occurrence of hyperactive and impulsive behavior by dyslexic boys is reported at a higher rate than that exhibited by dyslexic girls. The result is a disproportional referral rate. When girls display more aggressive behaviors that mirror those of males, it triggers the referral process and the subsequent diagnosis of a reading disability.

Gender Differences in Dyslexia

The mystery of dyslexia has taken a new twist as a recent study revealed brain differences in males and females with dyslexia (Olulade et al., 2013). By using MRI, neuroscientists at Georgetown University Medical Center found significant differences in brain anatomy when comparing men and women with dyslexia to their nondyslexic control groups. This is the first evidence that the condition may have different brain-based indicators based on sex. There is documented evidence of variance in brain anatomy. Females tend to use both hemispheres for language tasks, while males use just the left. It is also known that sex hormones are related to brain anatomy and that female sex hormones such as estrogen can be protective after brain injury.

The study of 118 participants compared the brain structure of people with dyslexia to those without and was conducted separately in men, women, boys, and girls. In males with dyslexia, less gray matter volume was found in areas of the brain used to process language, consistent with previous work. In females with dyslexia, less gray matter volume was found in areas involved in sensory and motor processing. Women with reading disabilities have distinct brain differences from men with reading disabilities. This suggests that existing male-based brain models of dyslexia may not apply to females with dyslexia. Major findings suggested that dyslexia may have different neural origins in each sex, raising the possibility that girls and boys may benefit from differential diagnosis and treatment. Future studies on sex differences in dyslexia need to examine brain function in order to get a more complete picture of how the reading disability develops.

Caveats

Unfortunately, there are charlatans who will take emotional and financial advantage of the desperate parents of the reading disabled. Providers of costly vision therapy require parents to commit to 60–90 hours of left to right tracking exercises at $90–$120 an hour. Trendy movement therapy promises improved balance in the body and the brain. The neighborhood chiropractor is more than willing to lead the dyslexic child through a series of exercises promised to improve reading performance. The well-meaning but misinformed reading specialist assures the parents that their child's reading will improve if only they use multicolored overlays on the child's reading materials. The correction of this very serious disability is not so simple. In order to effectively address the identification and remediation of dyslexic children, we must first protect the parents of these children from unnecessary expenditure of time and money by answering the question: Why can't my son read?

CHAPTER 3

Attention and Executive Function

When Ellen's sister turned 16, she was the lucky recipient of a red Ford Falcon convertible. You can imagine her excitement and Ellen's jealousy! There was one problem: It had a manual transmission. Neither sister knew how to master the coordination of letting off the clutch and pressing the gas while shifting the gears. They were undaunted by the challenge, and luckily, lived in a neighborhood with one road leading out. This provided a test driving track on which they could drive full circle without impediment or oncoming traffic.

The first attempt was an abject failure. Stall after stall after stall . . . Then Ellen's sister put the car in first gear and let off the clutch while pressing the gas pedal. It moved! It was a little jumpy, but it moved. They made it around the block without a single stall—all in first gear. They went to bed that night full of excitement. Then, the strangest thing happened. Ellen had a dream in which she drove the car effortlessly. It was like she had been driving a standard transmission all her life. When she awoke, she grabbed her sister and forced her to the car, pajamas and all, and took her place behind the wheel. It was exactly like the dream. Ellen drove through the neighborhood fluidly, moving through all four gears without a single stall.

When a task that formerly required attention for its performance can be performed without attention, the task is being done with automaticity. Automaticity in information processing means that information is processed with little attention. When Ellen woke and was able to fluidly drive the standard transmission without thinking about the process, she had reached automaticity.

Automaticity

Rabiner and Coie (2000) sought to determine whether attention problems predict the development of reading difficulties. They examined whether screening for attention problems could be of practical value in identifying children at risk for reading underachievement. Three hundred eighty-seven children were monitored from kindergarten through fifth grade. They were administered standardized assessments of attention problems and reading achievement at multiple time points.

Results indicated that attention problems predicted reading achievement even after controlling for prior reading achievement, IQ, and other behavioral difficulties. Inattentive first graders with normal reading scores after kindergarten were at risk for poor reading outcomes. Attention problems play an important role in the development of reading difficulties for some children, and screening for attention problems may help identify children at risk for reading difficulties.

The LaBerge-Samuels (LaBerge & Samuels, 1974) model of automatic information processing is one of the most widely quoted of all of the reading theories and emphasizes the role of attention in the reading process. It uses the concept of automaticity to explain why fluent readers are able to decode and understand text with ease while beginning readers and struggling readers have difficulty. Your son processes text through his visual and phonological memory systems. When automatic decoding occurs, he can finally comprehend the information in his semantic memory. This is the ultimate goal of reading.

There are three key components that serve to explain automaticity theory. The first concept is referred to as cognitive overload. As beginning or struggling readers attempt to read text, a disproportionate amount of their attention is spent decoding letters and words to the extent that they overload the cognitive capacity of their working memory. They are unable to move information into long-term memory and organize the meaning of what they are reading.

Fluent readers automatically decode, which frees up their working memory resources and enables them to attend to and comprehend what they are reading. Boys must master a system that enables them to automatically decode phonetically consistent words and perceive high-frequency words as holistic units. Once your son can automatically decode words, then he can focus his attention on employing strategies that will enable him to read with fluency and to comprehend what he reads.

Automaticity is the gold standard of reading. It is characterized by quick, correct, and effortless word recognition. The rate and precision at which single words are known is the best predictor of comprehension (Hook & Jones, 2002). It also allows your son to perform a reading task without significant demands on attention or memory (LaBerge & Samuels, 1974). Therefore, the development of skills necessary for increasing automaticity and fluency is vital (Hook & Jones, 2002).

Boys who do not achieve automaticity in decoding, comprehension, and attention will struggle with learning to read and will be unable to effectively connect with text. Struggling readers are often frustrated because they have laboriously gotten through the passage only to realize they cannot remember what they read. If your son is tenacious, he will reread the passage. Many struggling boys are not so persistent and will soon come to despise reading and ultimately avoid it altogether.

Cognitive Control

Cognitive control is the ability to move toward one's goals while simultaneously avoiding interference from influential distractors.

Cognitive control is a central component of memory (Baddeley & Hitch, 1974), attention, and general intelligence (Kyllonen & Christal, 1990). In addition, it is central to the process of learning to read. From a parent's perspective, the significant academic aspect of cognitive control is that it appears to be a major factor that distinguishes high achievers from underachievers.

Your son's resistance to interference reflects the effectiveness of his cognitive control. The precise processes he uses to minimize attention to the distraction are often unknown. Boys with strong cognitive control perceive subtle cues that allow them to adjust their attention before an interfering stimulus is encountered. This allows them to ignore the interference or at least minimize its influence. Your son is frequently faced with the challenge of reading an assignment in the face of distractions. It might be a Facebook page on a neighboring student's laptop or a disruptive student who just walked into the classroom. Once your son is familiar with his environment, he needs your help to learn to anticipate the occurrence of distractions and avoid falling victim to them.

Tips for Cognitive Control

Take the time to openly discuss the types of distractors your son is encountering. Ask him to be specific about who and what causes the distractions both at school and at home. Then go over the following tips to help him learn selective attention.

1. Develop a firm resolve. You son needs to develop a firm conviction that what he is doing needs to be done and he cannot waste any time. No matter how interesting that conversation is going on next to him, he needs to remember that his success depends on his ability to shut it out.

2. Don't confuse distraction with procrastination. Sometimes we complain that we are distracted and can't keep our focus on the reading assignment, but in actual fact we are just procrastinating. Make sure your son knows the difference.

3. Set a goal. Each day your son should set a reading goal. If he wants to get a book report done by the end of the day, he needs to set specific goals and write them down. Written goals are powerful.

4. Be strong. When the class clown starts his antics, it is easy to do what everyone else does. Breaking your concentration doesn't help you get your work done. Remind your son that he is in control of his mind and should be strong.

5. Be a rock, not a tree. The best student is a rock. He doesn't get blown around by the wind. Remind you son that if he allows external distractions to slow his process toward completing his goals, it will not be long before he will have lost control of his life. He should be like the rock.

6. Relax. When you son becomes too stressed, it is difficult to achieve any sort of focus. When he is relaxed, he is more able to focus, his thoughts will be clearer, and he will have more control over them. Here are a few suggestions:

1. Use deep, cleansing breaths.
2. Meditate.
3. Reach out to friends.
4. Be aware of the stress in each part of your body.
5. Quiet your mind and think only of your surroundings.

7. Disconnect the Internet, TV, iPod, Video Game . . . If your son needs to get his reading done, turn off all toys for an hour or so. Make sure he has everything he needs and then just switch them off for a specific amount of time. The mind is willing but the flesh is weak. If distractions are easily available, he will often fall victim to them. Know what distracts him and get rid of it before he starts reading.

8. Avoid the caffeine and sugar. Caffeine and sugar make us jittery and anxious. It is very hard to stay focused when you have had a few soft drinks. If your son needs to drink while reading, it is better to drink green tea, water, milk, or something that has a relaxing effect.

9. Close the door. Ask the family to leave your son alone if the door is closed. Post a sign that says READER AT WORK.

10. Find a deep motivation. When your son has a strong motivation, he will be more able to accomplish tasks in a meaningful way.

He must apply this motivation to every assignment and reading will become a very meaningful journey.

Attention Deficit/Hyperactivity Disorder (ADHD)

If repeated efforts to assist your son to strengthen his cognitive control result in failure and frustration, a more serious issue may be causing the problem. The fifth edition of the *Diagnostic and Statistical Manual of Mental Disorders* (DSM-5; American Psychiatric Association, 2013) characterized ADHD as a pattern of behavior, present in multiple settings, that can result in performance issues in social, educational, or work settings. There are two criteria for diagnosis. The first is inattention. The second is the combination of hyperactivity and impulsivity.

For your son to be diagnosed as ADHD, he must have at least six symptoms from either (or both) the inattention group of criteria and the hyperactivity and impulsivity criteria. The new DSM-5 designates ADHD symptoms must be present prior to age 12 years rather than the previous onset requirement of 7 years. In addition, the DSM-5 includes no exclusion criteria for those with autism spectrum disorder, because symptoms of both disorders can co-occur. However, there are exclusions related to ADHD symptoms that occur exclusively during the course of schizophrenia or another psychotic disorder. Additionally, behaviors must not be better explained by another mental disorder, such as a depressive or bipolar disorder, anxiety disorder, dissociative disorder, personality disorder, or substance intoxication or withdrawal.

Signs and Symptoms

Inattention, hyperactivity, and impulsivity are the key behaviors of ADHD. It is normal for all children to be inattentive, hyperactive, or impulsive sometimes, but for children with ADHD, these behaviors are more severe and occur more often. To be diagnosed with the disorder, a child must have symptoms for 6 or more months and to a degree that is greater than other children of the same age (National Institute of Mental Health, 2013). Boys who have symptoms of inattention may:

➤ be easily distracted, miss details, forget things, and frequently switch from one activity to another;

➤ have difficulty focusing attention on organizing and completing a task or learning something new;

➤ have trouble completing or turning in homework assignments, often losing things (e.g., pencils, folders, assignments) needed to complete tasks or activities;

➤ not seem to listen when spoken to;

➤ daydream, become easily confused, and move slowly;

➤ have difficulty processing information as quickly and accurately as others; and

➤ struggle to follow instructions.

Boys who have symptoms of hyperactivity may:

➤ fidget and squirm in their seats;

➤ talk nonstop;

➤ dash around, touching or playing with anything and everything in sight;

➤ have trouble sitting still during dinner, school, and story time;

➤ be constantly in motion; and

➤ have difficulty doing quiet tasks or activities.

Boys who have symptoms of impulsivity may:

➤ be very impatient;

➤ blurt out inappropriate comments, show their emotions without restraint, and act without regard for consequences;

➤ have difficulty waiting for things they want or waiting for turns in games; and

➤ often interrupt conversations or others' activities.

Causes of ADHD

Members of the National Institute for Mental Health (NIMH, 2013) reported that they are still uncertain as to the causes of ADHD. Many studies suggest that genes play a large role, but like so many other illnesses, ADHD probably results from a combination of genetics, environmental factors, brain injuries, nutrition, and the social environment.

Genes. Twins studies show that ADHD often runs in families. Researchers at NIMH are searching for the genes involved so that prevention of the disorder could one day become a reality. Learning about specific genes could also lead to better treatments.

Environmental factors. There are several possible environmental links to ADHD. Some studies suggest a potential link between ADHD and cigarette and alcohol use during pregnancy. Preschoolers who are exposed to high levels of lead may have a higher risk of developing ADHD.

Brain injuries. A small percentage of children with ADHD have suffered a traumatic brain injury.

Food additives. There is ongoing research searching for a possible link between consumption of certain food additives and an increase in activity. Research seeks to confirm the findings and to learn more about how food additives may affect hyperactivity.

Diagnosis of ADHD

ADHD symptoms usually appear between the ages of 3 and 6. Often, teachers notice the symptoms first, when a child has trouble following rules or frequently "spaces out" in the classroom or on the playground.

Because there is no single test to diagnose ADHD, the pediatrician or mental health specialist will first try to rule out other possibilities for the symptoms, such as:

> ➤ a middle ear infection that is causing hearing problems;
> ➤ undetected hearing or vision problems;
> ➤ medical problems that affect thinking and behavior;
> ➤ learning disabilities;

> ➤ anxiety or depression, or other psychiatric problems that might cause ADHD-like symptoms;
> ➤ a significant and sudden change, such as the death of a family member, a divorce, or a parent's job loss;
> ➤ home or school settings that appear unusually stressful or disrupted;
> ➤ whether behaviors are continuous problem or a response to a temporary situation; or
> ➤ whether behaviors occur in several settings or only in one place, such as the playground, classroom, or home.

Treatment for Boys With ADHD

Current treatments for ADHD include medication, psychotherapy, education or training, or a combination of treatments. Carefully administered and monitored treatments can improve ADHD symptoms, but there is no cure. With treatment, boys with ADHD can learn to read, be successful in school, and lead productive lives. Advanced technology provides hope for more effective treatments and interventions. New tools such as brain imaging provide the opportunity to better understand ADHD and to find more effective ways to treat and prevent it.

Medications. The most common type of medication used for treating ADHD is called a stimulant. Although it is counterintuitive to treat ADHD with a a stimulant, it has a calming effect on children with ADHD. Other ADHD medications are nonstimulants and work differently than stimulants. For many children, ADHD medications improve hyperactivity and impulsivity and the ability to focus, work, and learn.

Every child with ADHD is different; consequently, a one-size-fits-all approach does not apply for children with ADHD. Your son might have side effects with a certain medication, while another child may not. This is the time to be patient and work with your physician because several different medications or dosages must be tried before finding one that works for your son.

ADHD medications come in different forms. Medications are short-acting, long-acting, or extended release. The active ingredient is the same, but it is released differently in the body. Parents and doctors should decide together which medication is best for the child and whether the child needs medication only for school hours or for other aspects of their lives.

Do medications cure ADHD? Current medications do not cure ADHD. They control the symptoms for as long as they are taken. Medications can help a child pay attention and complete schoolwork. It is not clear, however, whether medications can help children learn or improve their academic skills. Adding behavioral therapy, counseling, and practical support can help children with ADHD and their families better cope with everyday problems. Research funded by the National Institute of Mental Health (2013) has shown that medication works best when treatment is regularly monitored by the prescribing doctor and the dose is adjusted based on the child's needs.

Psychotherapy. There are several types of psychotherapy used for ADHD. Behavioral therapy is used to help your son change his behavior. It often involves hands-on assistance with organizing tasks or completing schoolwork. Behavioral therapy also teaches a child how to monitor his or her own behavior through praise or rewards for acting in a desired way. Parents and teachers also can assist with this process by giving positive or negative feedback for certain behaviors. In addition, clear rules, chore lists, and other structured routines can help a child control his or her behavior.

Therapists may teach children social skills, such as how to wait their turn, share toys, ask for help, or respond to teasing. Learning to read facial expressions and the tone of voice in others and how to respond appropriately can also be part of social skills training (NIMH, 2013).

ADHD and the Family

Sometimes, the whole family may need to get involved. ADHD affects the entire family and family members need to find better ways to handle disruptive behaviors and to encourage behavior changes.

This can occur through family therapy, support groups, and chat rooms. Talking with other parents and families who have similar problems and concerns often proves to be helpful. The following websites offer specific sources for support and practical ideas:

> ➤ http://www.chadd.org
> ➤ http://www.ldonline.org
> ➤ http://www.add.org
> ➤ http://www.kidshealth.org/parents/emotions/behavior/ adhd.html

When your son enters school, his ADHD behaviors will become apparent to his teacher. His interactions with other kids in a school setting might bring out some of those ADHD behaviors in ways that challenge his teachers. If your son's behavior challenges become an issue, they can be addressed with a reward plan. A well-thought-out reward plan can help you help your son establish desirable behaviors. Carefully think through any management plan. If it is going to work, everyone must commit to being consistent in its use. Consider the following six steps:

1. **Identify the problem behavior(s).** Work with your son on this one. When boys begin school, undesirable behaviors can seem multiplied. Talk to your son's teacher, then sit down with your son and discuss what you and his teachers expect from him. It is important to begin work on only one behavior at a time so your son can focus. The older the child, the more behaviors you can work on at once.

2. **Select a fun behavior chart.** You can find a behavior chart at http://www.kidpointz.com to print out and hang on the wall. Again, get your son's input so that he feels in control of the process. Use check marks or award points when he reaches each goal. Change the format of the chart each week. It's also okay to raise the bar and make the behavior task a bit more challenging. For example, if you're working on listening behavior, instead of giving a point for each time he pays attention instead of interrupting you, offer 5 points if he listens each day that week at home and at school. Set up

an online system for computer-oriented kids to keep track of behavior points.

3. **Select a reward.** Make sure that the reward is commensurate with the behavior you're working on. Save larger rewards for more challenging behaviors; use smaller rewards for small goals. Let the teacher decide the rewards that work best for her classroom.

4. **Follow through.** No behavior or reward plan will work unless you follow through. A behavior chart is designed to keep you and your child on task. For elementary aged kids, put the chart in a conspicuous place; keep charts for older kids in a notebook. Stay on top of the plan and your child will follow suit.

5. **Recognition.** Make reward day a big deal. Give your child plenty of praise.

Involve as many individuals as you can in your son's behavioral plan. Most importantly, involve your son in every step of the process to ensure his participation.

For more information on helping your son overcome the negative aspects of ADHD, see *Raising Boys With ADHD: Secrets for Parenting Healthy, Happy Sons* (Forgan & Richey, 2012).

Executive Dysfunction and Reading

Prepare yourself for the first time you hear that your first-grade son struggles with executive functions. This new educational jargon is becoming more common in parent conferences across the country. Executive functions are the essential self-regulating skills that boys use every day to accomplish just about everything. They help them plan, organize, make decisions, shift between situations or thoughts, control their emotions and impulsivity, and learn from past mistakes. Boys rely on their executive functions for everything from taking a shower to packing a backpack.

Children who have poor executive functioning, including many with ADHD, are more disorganized than other kids. They might take longer to get dressed or avoid simple chores around the house. Notebooks are filled with loose papers, and it is common to start week-long assignments the night before they are due.

Does this sound familiar? "Do you have homework? Have you done your homework? Where is your homework? Have you started your summer reading? You have to clean up your room! How can you find anything in that book bag? Is that last week's lunch in there? Are you listening to me? Do I need to tell you again? This is the last time I am going to remind you to put your book bag by the door before you go to bed." Do you ask a question and get an answer that's related but not quite connected to the question? Don't assume these behaviors are intentional defiance.

Don't call him lazy. Boys who lack motivation to read or who are struggling readers are often described as lazy, intentionally forgetful, unmotivated, deliberately late, disorganized, and sometimes opposi-tional. Adults engaging in this type of "blaming the victim" behavior need to realize the damage they are doing. Executive functions begin in infancy and include attention, inhibition, working memory, and cognitive flexibility. These processes provide the means by which indi-viduals control their own behavior, work toward goals, and manage complex cognitive processes.

Executive function plays a critical role in the development of read-ing. The development of executive function in young children involves changes in brain structures that occur with growth. Because execu-tive function and its associated brain developments parallel reading acquisition, it is essential to understand their profound implications for nurturing the successful development of reading skills. This process begins as early as preschool when boys are acquiring prereading skills. Executive functions continue to impact the successful word reading and reading comprehension of the older reader.

There are two stages of executive function development. The first stage is the apprentice stage. During this stage, children begin the process of developing early reading skills. The five core developing processes are comprehension, phonological awareness, fluency, vocabulary, and phonics. Growing competence in these early literacy concepts is predictive of students' later reading achievement (Neuman & Dickinson, 2001; Snow, Burns, & Griffin, 1998). In the middle grades, your son moves into the master stage of executive function development. Goals are a major focus and become complex. Reading skills become automatic and enable boys to build confidence because goal attainment seems effortless.

The 10 Executive Functions

1. **Inhibition of impulses.** Inhibition is the intention to resist impulses and to stop one's behavior at the appropriate time. It is the ability to voluntarily control a response; to think before you act. It is one of many executive functions that exist in the frontal cortex of the brain.

2. **Sustaining attention.** Sustained attention, or vigilance, as it is more often called, refers to the state in which attention must be maintained over time. Reading comprehension requires sustained attention or information read will never make it to long-term memory, where it will be organized and ready for further manipulation.

3. **Shifting attention.** Moving the focus of attention from one thing to another—for example, from a video game to homework.

4. **Emotional control.** The ability to manage emotions in order to achieve goals, complete tasks, or control and direct behavior. When a teen has difficulties with emotional control, it may present in some of the following ways:
   - ➢ difficulty with competition: athletic or academic;
   - ➢ difficulty handling change in plans;
   - ➢ hard time taking the word "no" for an answer;
   - ➢ not handling criticism well;
   - ➢ feeling anxious before a test; and
   - ➢ initiating activity planning and defining the first step (*Note*: This causes problems with initiation of the activity especially writing).

5. **Planning.** A student may have problems with executive function when he or she has trouble planning projects.

6. **Organization.** Organizing and planning are frequently used interchangeably, but actually they are different. Poor organization suggests things are not properly sequenced whereas poor planning means things are not properly anticipated.

7. **Self-Monitoring.** Students often have difficulty self-monitoring effectively and they do not check or correct their work efficiently. These weaknesses are often even more pronounced in students who have learning or attention difficulties. They often lose sight of their goals and objectives, they may not select the best strategies for specific tasks, and they cannot easily find their errors. Instead, they often spend many hours working and may become increasingly frustrated because they:

   ➢ may be unaware of the approaches they are using to complete their work;

   ➢ may not recognize when they are feeling "stuck" and need to shift to an alternate approach to complete their work because they are not independently monitoring and adjusting the strategies they use; or

   ➢ may not know how to check or correct their errors independently.

8. **Time management.** For the student, time management is the examination and determination of how their waking/studying hours are spent or how they rank the tasks that they need to do to get then done in the most effective and productive way possible.

9. **Conceptualization.** Conceptualization is the ability to mentally manipulate ideas, experiences, structures, relationships, etc.

10. **Working memory.** Working memory is a system for temporarily storing and managing the information required to carry out complex cognitive tasks such as learning, reasoning, and comprehension. Working memory is involved in the selection,

initiation, and termination of information-processing functions such as encoding, storing, and retrieving data. As information comes in, you're processing it at the same time as you store it. A child uses this skill when doing math calculations or listening to a story. He has to hold onto the numbers while working with them. Or, he needs to remember the sequence of events and also think of what the story is about. Working memory is the foundation of the brain's executive functions. But if you struggle with working memory, pieces of information may slip through your fingers before having the opportunity to grasp the concept.

The mastery stage of executive function is not always achieved at the developmentally appropriate time. As a result, the early reading skills have not been mastered and effortless reading has not been achieved. The foundations for learning to read are attention, memory, and executive function, so it is surprising that executive dysfunction is an often-overlooked source of difficulty with and resistance to reading. Boys with executive dysfunction suffer from inattention, poor planning and organizational skills, memory deficits, emotional instability, and poor self-monitoring. With this understanding, we can begin to help boys develop the reading-specific executive functions during the apprenticeship stage that will enable them to manage the complexities of reading processes throughout their lives.

Success Strategies for Executive Dysfunction

Strategy #1: Define expectations. Before a student begins to work on an assignment, have him create a checklist of expectations using the following questions:

➢ How many pages should it be?

➢ What will he be graded on? Is there a rubric available?

➢ Is there a defined structure (i.e., lab report, five paragraph essay, etc.)?

➢ When is it due?

When he has completed the assignment, the student can then use his checklist to be sure that he has met expectations.

Strategy #2: Test preparation. When a student starts to study for a test, he should:

➢ assemble old assignments, quizzes, notes, and handouts;

➢ create a list of the errors that he made; and

➢ check for emerging patterns. If there is a particular concept that he is consistently missing or a careless error that keeps rearing its ugly head, it might be time for a few sessions with a tutor before the test.

When he begins the test, he should write any "errors to avoid" in the upper left corner to remind him of what to check when he has completed the test.

Strategy #3: Keep a record of performance. Success will mean different things for different students. Grades might be a good way to track progress. However, you might need to define success in smaller achievable tasks so that you son can see improvement. Such tasks might include:

➢ Keep a running list of grades.

➢ Post a homework checklist and place a check by completed assignments.

➢ Create a graph of minutes spent reading every day for a visual of progress.

➢ Create a calendar and a to-do list for each long-term assignment.

Strategy #4: Provide instruction before, during, and after. In order to set students up for success, we need them to have strategies that they can employ before an assignment, while completing an assignment, and after the assignment is done. These include:

➢ making a plan for locating all information, textbooks, pencils, computer, etc.;

➢ knowing what behaviors are expected while he works on the assignment. How often should he take a break? In what order should he complete the assignment?; and

> ➤ finally, after an assignment is completed, work needs to be checked and cleaned up. This is when proofreading is done and revisions made. Then book bags are cleaned out and the new assignments are placed carefully in the appropriate folder.

Strategy #5: Provide visual cues. Once your son has found the strategies that work for him, it is time to create a visual reminder to employ these strategies. This could be a poster to represent planning, doing, and checking. He might create a poster with a mnemonic device or acrostic poem to help him remember the steps to go through. This poster should be put right above his work space, with a smaller version in his notebook.

Strategy #6: Setting up the workspace. An organized workspace helps children to find the materials they need for homework easily and independently. Storing materials in different sections is always helpful. For example, all writing tools should be located together (e.g., pens, pencils, erasers, markers), as should all papers (e.g., blank, ruled, graph). Keep reference materials, including calculators, dictionaries, and atlases, close to your child's homework workspace. Help your child to identify a regular time during the week for clearing out and organizing his or her backpack. Work together to make this a pleasant experience so that it becomes a habit. Encourage your child to use a brightly colored pocket folder to transport important papers. Keep a ready supply of graphic organizers either electronically or on paper.

These strategies are important stepping stones to independence, but in the beginning you will need to work as partners. If you feel that sets up a stressful relationship, hire a tutor to work through these strategies until your son can accomplish them on his own. The eventual goal is for a student to be able to evaluate an assignment on his own and complete the work.

The deficits associated with executive dysfunction can be in the form of difficulty in organizing time, difficulty in organizing materials and belongings, difficulty in organizing thoughts, difficulty in initiating tasks, difficulty in switching flexibly between tasks, difficulty in sustaining focus on the relevant aspects of a stimulus or task, or any combination of these skills. If your son suffers from these behaviors, it's time to have him assessed for executive dysfunction.

CHAPTER 4

Competition and Motivation

Reluctant readers will respond best to your efforts to get them reading for pleasure if you can present reading in a fun way. Your son might be more motivated when faced with a challenge. Although popular reading competitions are often (and rightly) criticized for substituting extrinsic rewards for what ought to be an intrinsically enjoyable experience, we believe that a carefully designed competition *can* promote genuine love of reading.

Mixing reading with competition is a combination to which boys are likely to respond. Boys shy away from reading largely from insecurity, the feeling that this is not the right thing for them to do. In our culture, reading is sometimes not seen as a "masculine" activity. A well-designed reading challenge can counter this insecurity if the goals are kept in mind. We must convince boys that reading is an acceptable activity and that reading in quantity is, in itself, success (Sullivan, 2003).

Considerable thought should go into designing a competition that offers meaningful incentives while avoiding the harmful potential side effects, such as lowering students' self-esteem. A poorly designed competition will give your son negative associations with reading, just as, say, being paid to read a book that never captures his interest leaves him with the impression that reading is not intrinsically valuable.

Your son will eventually like to read if he is introduced to the right material, but you may need to work with external incentives until he stumbles on the internal rewards for himself. After all, he can't enjoy reading if he never reads in the first place. He's also unlikely to enjoy it if he only reads when forced. Try using the carrot rather than the stick whenever possible. For example, he will probably be less open to the possibility of enjoying his book if you're making him read until he finishes a certain number of pages. This may seem like a good idea, but keep in mind that if he's turning pages so he'll be allowed to put the book down when he's done, *not* reading becomes the payoff of reading. That's the opposite of what you want him to think! Reading should be its own reward. If your son lacks intrinsic motivation at first, then a positive extrinsic motivation (e.g., extra video game time on the weekend) is better than a negative one (e.g., no video games until reading grades improve). In other words, it's better for him to view reading as a means to an end than as an obstacle to his desires.

But what is the most appropriate bait for a reluctant reader? What challenges will stimulate his best efforts without reinforcing a negative learner identity? A number of programs exist to incentivize reading, but before you can evaluate their usefulness for your son, there are some basic facts about competition that you should know.

The Scoop on Competition

Despite the mocking that our school culture of "everyone gets a ribbon" receives, parents and educators are justified in their concern about the effects of competition on children. Potential negative outcomes include the following (Kohn, 1992):

> ➢ Competition can harm self-esteem. Most people lose in a competition. Winners aren't off the hook either; they can only be winners if they continue to beat everyone else.

> ➢ Children succeed in spite of competition. There are 65 studies over a 60-year period that show that children learn better when they work together and worse when they compete.
> ➢ Competition may create hostility. Think about when that pitcher throws his hat on the ground after pitching a home run. Or the constant fighting in all sports. When people get behind, they get frustrated.
> ➢ Most telling, collaborative styles of teaching are proven to be way more effective for learning than competitive styles.

We must be aware that extreme competition can devastate a child. Temperament, culture, talent, and the age of the child can all affect how he handles competition. You know your child. Focus on his temperament. He may thrive on competition, or he may become a nervous wreck when he is compared to others. You need to treat your child as the individual that he is. There is no need to push an already competitive child to compete, but it may be appropriate to encourage a more reluctant child who shows potential.

Researchers have uncovered a number of interesting factors at play in competitions that should inform your judgment in selecting appropriate challenges for your son. The following paragraphs provide a quick guide to the most pertinent information for parents of reluctant readers, but for more on this topic, we recommend *Top Dog: The Science of Winning and Losing* (Bronson & Merryman, 2013).

The principle of close races. When a contest is close, this induces extra effort from the competitors, who feel they have a chance to win. When a contest is not close, competition does not bring about extra effort or improved performance. Picture the spelling bee with the entire class looking on. The speller with dyslexia knows he doesn't have a chance. This is the perfect time to make a trip to see the nurse.

Boys will get more excited about a contest if they have a fighting chance to win. Almost any contest can be altered to remove excessive ability gaps between competitors. Instead of a traditional whole-class or whole-grade spelling bee, for example, teachers and administrators might consider dividing the class or grade by reading level or by previously demonstrated spelling performance and rewarding the top performers in each group. This adjustment transforms the spelling bee from an opportunity for great spellers to show off while the others slouch and pray for it to be over, to an opportunity for all students to improve skills through increased effort.

Risk–reward bias. Those who focus on the risks of competing give little thought to the potential rewards of that risk. Those who focus on the reward see too little of the risk. Analysis of risk versus reward is often influenced by a person's gender. On average, women are biased to analyze the odds while men are biased to focus on the rewards. Some of the more dramatic consequences of risk–reward bias are that women shy away from running for Congress, but make better stock analysts on Wall Street.

Enter your son's mind as he makes decisions regarding whether to study for the test or go to the skate park with his friends. For a young man, the risk of failing a test probably seems more remote and less important than the instant reward of doing something he enjoys. As a parent, you might reflect on the personal experiences that did the most to teach you self-discipline and the value of delayed gratification. What might you do to create similar experiences for your son? What might you say to enhance his sense of the risks involved in a bad decision or the rewards of making a good one? Is there a more immediate or more important (to him) reward you might offer for wise decisions?

Warriors and worriers. Genetic variability in the COMT enzyme, the enzyme that clears dopamine from the prefrontal cortex, leads to two types of people. Those with the warrior genotype perform better under stress. Those with the worrier genotype perform better in the absence of stress (i.e., under normal circumstances). Knowing your son's disposition as a warrior or worrier should guide the types of competitions in which he should participate. It is important to resist labeling one genotype as better than the other; both have associated strengths and drawbacks. Let your son's teacher know the types of competitions that facilitate his academic improvement and those that will send him running in the opposite direction.

The key to appropriate selection of academic competitions for both warriors and worriers is insight into the students' levels of perceived self-efficacy in relation to the competition. Each boy's belief in his ability to overcome external variables in order to produce a desired outcome should determine your instructional course of action. Worriers need the security of competitive activities that are demanding but structured in such a way that success seems attainable. This can be accomplished by providing a well defined rubric or checklist that details the path to success. Having a long time to practice or work on their competitive project, as opposed to an on-the-spot performance, might benefit this type. Warriors also need to believe that achievement is attainable, but they might feel more comfortable with a rapidly approaching deadline or lack of prescribed rules and guidelines. Amping up the pressure of the competition amps up their performance.

The stress-performance sweet spot. Competition is always stressful, and we cannot habituate to it. But stress does not necessarily impair performance. If the mind interprets the stress as beneficial, then the increased arousal actually helps performance. Ellen has found that competition with a timer enhances a performer's focus. This is especially effective with fluency activities.

All of Ellen's students love "The 60 Second Challenge," in which they compete against themselves to read words off PowerPoint slides. Ellen's PowerPoint provides 60 examples of the decoding pattern. Figure 4.1 shows an example.

You can also set up a timed competition for your son by creating a PowerPoint containing the words that focus on his problematic decoding pattern. When making your own, place one word on each slide. For the first round, set the transition time at 5-second intervals between slides. If your son is struggling at the 4-second mark, say the word and proceed to the next. Keep a record of how many words he reads in 60 seconds. If the results are disappointing, engaging in untimed practice followed by a redo usually brings a more successful score. Thirty words at 60 seconds is the sweet spot. Once your son can read 30 words, reduce the timer by one second.

The audience–performance inversion. Why does it sometimes help, and sometimes hurt, to perform in front of an audience? When your son performs something he has mastered, he experiences a rush of exhilaration. Knowing he is watched increases this feeling.

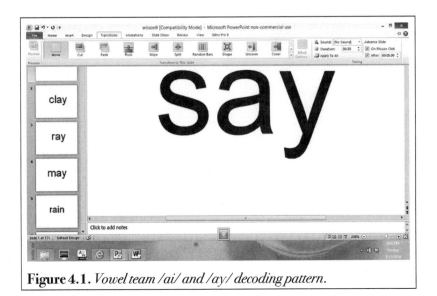

Figure 4.1. *Vowel team /ai/ and /ay/ decoding pattern.*

The opposite is true, however, when he is still learning. When he has not fully mastered a skill, having an audience makes his performance decline.

Ellen's best tool for sheltered performance is a karaoke machine. She uses the record function with a monitor that plays back for an audience of one. You can get the same result for your son by recording him with a cell phone or tablet with a video option and tracking his progress.

The power of rivalry. This term describes the additional focus and effort brought to bear when competing against someone with whom you have a lot in common, especially when you face them on a recurring basis. The best person for your son to compete against is himself. Develop a system to track his progress in various reading activities (such as those described in Chapter 6) and provide rewards at important milestones.

If your son is 13 years of age or older, consider having him sign up for a Goodreads account at http://www.goodreads.com. Bringing a social media element into the reading experience may appeal to him, as the site would allow him to discuss his favorite reading materials with people who share his taste and discover new books that appeal to him. But perhaps most importantly, Goodreads provides an easy, convenient way to record all of the books he reads and automatically tracks his progress toward whatever reading goal he sets.

The goal looms larger effect. As an individual or a team gets closer to completing its goal—or closer to the end of the game—this changes motivation and mental strategy. The nearness of the finish line causes some to turn it up a notch. Graphing individual performance data adds to the motivation of the learner. This can be done with graph paper in a notebook. Display publicly only if that is suggested by your son.

The N effect. This is the tendency to lose motivation when faced with a large field of competitors. It's part of the reason that setting individual goals and competing against oneself is so effective. In situations when competing against other people is necessary or desirable, it might be helpful to try to ignore the presence of competitors to whatever extent possible. If your son's contest takes the form of a written test, encourage him to get a seat at the front of the room where he can't see his competition.

The diamagnetic property of teams. Teams repel stars because stars want to be recognized for their individual performance. Stars don't want to apply for jobs that have "teamwork" in the description, because they worry that their teammates will ride on their individual effort and success.

Your son may have had the experience of being the last chosen because of his reading challenges. He may also have taken advantage of the knowledge of others. Neither of these outcomes are beneficial to your son. Encourage him to work individually or with other students who share similar strengths and weaknesses. Discuss this preference with his teacher.

The bad winner. People talk about the "bad loser," but this same person is probably also a bad winner. Whether he wins or loses, he thinks he's entitled to the win, doesn't respect his opponent, and isn't motivated to improve his skills. Don't rely on platitudes, however true, to teach your son good beliefs about competition. "Sometimes you win, sometimes you lose" isn't going to cut it here. For better or worse, competition is too prevalent in our society to ignore this aspect of your child's development.

The model you provide of being a good winner and loser will set the stage for your son's reaction to the outcomes of competition. When you hear him make the types of statements characteristic of "bad" competitors, gently guide to him to a better attitude by asking thought-provoking questions. "Why do you think Billy 'didn't deserve' to win? Do you think you would feel differently about that if you were Billy?" We are all born with some sense that we are the center of the universe and deserve or need the validation of winning, but learning to consider the perspectives of all involved—including rivals and judges—will benefit your son more in the long run than winning a particular contest ever could.

Additive thinking. After a setback, subtractive thinking is expressing regret for what didn't work out ("If only I'd made that shot"). In contrast, additive thinking is contemplating alternative strategies that you did not try, but that could be useful next time ("I should drive to the hoop rather than settle for that shot"). This is a skill and mindset that should be taught. The important question is how your son will react to academic setbacks. Your voice needs to lead the way in articulating some different study strategies that might provide a more positive outcome. Then jump in with him to try that new strategy and keep a record of its effectiveness.

Major Reading Competitions

Unfortunately, many of the most popular competitive reading programs used in this country encompass the harmful aspects of competition, or the ways they are often used in specific schools encompass the harmful aspects. For example, many schools that use the Accelerated Reader program offer a grand prize for the reader with the most points, which does nothing to motivate struggling readers. This violates the principle of close races. After reading about the most common reading competitions used in schools today, consider whether they are right for your son. If your school is using a reading competition that you feel is bad for your son, bring your concerns to his teacher. You may be able to get the administration to reconsider the program, and at the least you should be able to opt out your son.

Battle of the Books

In Battle of the Books competitions, all of the questions begin with the words "In which book . . .", and the correct answer is always the title and author of the book. Students read a set list of books, discuss them, quiz each other on the contents, and then compete in teams at the "Battle" to answer questions in a quiz show format. Questions are fairly straightforward, focusing on plot, characters, and setting.

This program motivates strong young readers to read more, but probably does not motivate kids who dislike reading. Because the focus is on fact recall, it can improve a reader's comprehension and retention, but may not enhance their interpretive and critical skills or their appreciation for the texts. Luckily, participation is voluntary. If you think the contest might benefit your son, learn how to get involved at http://www.battleofthebooks.org.

Accelerated Reader

In *The New York Times Book Review*, Susan Straight (2009) critiqued the omnipresent Accelerated Reading Program. Accelerated Reader was introduced in 1986. Renaissance Learning (2014; http://www. renaissance.com/) owns the program and described it as a way to build a lifelong love of reading and learning. Straight did not agree with this purported outcome as she attended back-to-school night one fall. She walked into the meeting prepared to confront her daughter's eighth-grade language arts teacher about the rise of Accelerated Reader.

The configuration of this reading management software system is designed to help teachers track student reading through computerized comprehension tests. Awards are given to students based on the points for books they read. The number of points received is based on length and difficulty of the selected book. This is standardized by using a readability rating (Renaissance Learning, 2014).

Straight never had the opportunity to confront her daughter's teacher. The teacher announced during the class presentation that she refused to use the AR program. This is an exception to the rule. AR is currently used in more than 75,000 schools from prekindergarten through 12th grade.

CHAPTER 5

Mistaught

The National Council on Teacher Quality (NCTQ, 2013) recently issued its review of U.S. schools of education. The 2013 Teacher Prep Review provided a look at how teachers are trained through our university system before they enter the classroom. According to the report, the "reading wars" are far from over. Three out of four elementary teacher preparation programs are still not teaching the methods of reading instruction that could substantially lower the number of children who never become proficient readers—from 30% to fewer than 10%. Instead, the teacher candidate is all too often told to develop his or her "own unique approach." These unique approaches are, unfortunately, often informed by misconceptions about reading instruction, including the following (Moats, 1999):

- reading instruction is only needed until third grade;
- competent teachers do not use published reading programs;
- avoiding published reading programs empowers teachers and enhances the professional status of teaching;
- teaching phonics, word identification, and spelling skills directly to children is harmful;
- those who favor good code instruction are opposed to literature and comprehension instruction;

> ➢ reading a lot is the best way to overcome a reading problem;
> ➢ children should be taught to guess words on the basis of meaning and syntax; and
> ➢ skills must always be taught in the context of literature.

Mastery of literacy as process requires that reading teachers understand the overall system of language (Snow & Juel, 2005). Expertise in phonological awareness, phonemic awareness, comprehension, vocabulary, and fluency provide the foundational components of a successful reading practice. In addition to providing instruction in these essential areas, the reading teacher must also address the confounding effects of motivation, attention deficit, and linguistic diversity.

The laissez-faire way in which reading teachers are prepared in 75% of our colleges of education creates the likelihood that at each subsequent grade level the reading achievement gap widens. In 1987, Dr. Thomas Armstrong coined the word *dysteachia* to refer to children suffering from inappropriate teaching strategies. We must acknowledge that there is dysteachia—that some kids have mislearned because they have been mistaught. I've never seen a boy with an IQ in the average range who couldn't be taught to read. They can all be taught to read if you start at the right level and you provide a sequence that teaches reading systematically.

Although various reasons have been suggested for reading problems, inadequate environment and poor reading instruction are at the top of the list. Environmental explanations of poor reading achievement include limited opportunities for adequate oral language development, lack of access to text material in the home, and few parental models of engagement in literacy activities. Instructional limitations include ineffective instructional methods performed by teachers lacking basic knowledge about the reading process.

There has been a tremendous amount of concern that students from high-risk home environments come to school less prepared for literacy than their more advantaged peers. The impact of poorly prepared teachers supersedes high-risk environments as a perpetrator of creating and exacerbating reading difficulties. The pervasiveness of this lack of teacher preparation is exemplified by a survey that was administered to 89 reading teachers, special education teachers, and speech-language pathologists (Moats, 1994). Responses to the survey indicated an inadequate understanding of language concepts and persistent weaknesses related to the concepts of the very skills needed for direct, language-focused reading instruction. Furthermore, few of these individuals could identify examples of the basic reading components taught in the primary grades. The conclusion from this survey is that "Ignorance was the norm" (Moats, 1994, p. 93).

Several other studies have utilized a similar questionnaire format. For instance, Bos, Mather, Dickson, Podhajski, and Chard (2001) examined the linguistic knowledge of preservice and in-service teachers using two separate questionnaires. The first measured teachers' knowledge of early reading and spelling instruction, and the other measured basic linguistic knowledge. Both preservice and in-service teachers had scores that fell below the 33rd percentile. In-service teachers believed that poor phonemic awareness contributed to early reading failure, but two thirds of the participants could not correctly define phonemic awareness. Preservice and in-service educators indicated that they strongly believed that K–2 teachers should know how to teach phonics, but the same teachers' responses to phonics-based questions indicated that they lacked the basic knowledge necessary to teach phonics. Teachers also overestimated their knowledge of reading and were unaware of what they knew and did not know.

The professionals from whom you seek help for your struggling son may not have the skills or knowledge to provide the help you so desperately need. Faced with this realization, you must arm yourself with the information to both teach and advocate for your son.

The Reading Wars Continue

There are two adversarial positions in the "reading wars," phonics versus whole language. It is hard to find anything on which the sides agree. One side insists we teach kids to read, while the other just as strongly asserts that as we expose kids to books, they learn to read.

The fundamental issue is whether reading education should focus primarily on the whole or the parts of reading. Phonics advocates support the teaching of a systematic, sequential decoding system that includes phonemic awareness, phonics, fluency, vocabulary, and comprehension. The whole language supporters are steadfast in their belief that the best way to motivate kids to read is to immerse them in written language. There's a lot of reading aloud by both students and teachers, using books chosen more on the basis of literary merit than whether all the words are systematically decodable. Kids are also asked to write their own stories and essays in which correct spelling is incidental. Instead of sounding out unknown words, whole language advocates typically ask the child to guess an unfamiliar word based on the context. If the word is reasonably close, the reading proceeds. The problem with word guessing is that the word is often wrong and this has a detrimental effect on comprehension.

The Dark Ages of Reading Instruction

Proponents of whole language dominate colleges of education. They refuse to budge on the issue that, because humans learn to speak their native language through immersion, the act of reading follows a similar pattern, and exposure to the printed word leads to the development of reading skills. The flaw with this theory is that in speech, the listener is provided with many clues as to the meaning of the words presented by the speaker. These include intonation, pitch, cadence, and body language. These elements provide powerful context clues that assist in the comprehension of auditory signals. Barring neurologically based developmental delays, children do not require explicit instruction to master the spoken language. This means speech is a natural process, but reading is not.

Reading involves a different process than speaking. Written language is a relatively recent human construct. In the evolution of writing, each of the world's languages has designated its own symbols to represent the sounds of spoken language. The sound-symbol correspondence that has been developed for the English language is called the alphabetic code.

The two key components of reading, which do not occur in speech, are word identification and concept imagery. Word identification involves recognizing that words are a systematic string of individual *graphemes*, or letters. Each individual sequential combination represents a different word. Students must be able to string together the individual phonemes (sounds) to produce these words. This is the essence of decoding. The other half of the reading puzzle involves comprehension of the meanings behind the sequential combinations of letters (words). Concept imagery allows students to visualize the item or process represented by the words. Students who have weak word identification skills will stumble and stammer as they attempt to read the printed language. Those weak in concept imagery—comprehension—may read with prosody but will not understand what was read.

We now know that whole language advocates were wrong; in fact, they have been wrong for three decades. They were only able to maintain their error because the philosophy that spawned whole language included opposition not only to teaching basic phonics skills, but also to testing those skills. By refusing to properly test the outcomes of their practices, educators hid the failure of whole language.

The whole language assertion that learning to read is the same process as learning to speak has long been ridiculed by researchers. Speech is a universal, instinctive process; nearly everyone can speak. But reading is not a natural process; it is learned. Reading is an unnatural process that we challenge the mind to undertake.

One of the leading advocates of whole language guessing practices was Kenneth Goodman. He once described reading as a "psycholinguistic guessing game" (Goodman, 1967). The whole language advocates in education departments of American universities still remain in control of teacher training. They still refuse to accept any contrary evidence. Many introductory reading courses have gone to an online format and provide teachers with little more than busy work and an emphasis on critical literacy rather than reading instruction. They do this because this is all they know. University instructors were never taught how to teach a child to read because most are products of the philosophy of whole language instruction. Most left the classrooms themselves and have little hands-on knowledge of how difficult it is to teach a child to read. This is not mere hindsight; researchers had been issuing warnings right from the outset . . . the evidence and the science was simply ignored for almost three decades.

I meet many teachers-in-training and have yet to meet one trainee who has a working knowledge of the linguistic foundations of learning to read. They complain that their literacy classes focus on social justice rather than improvement of literacy skills. It is up to you to fill in the instruction gap with a strong knowledge of how children learn to read.

Boys who are blessed with efficient processing of text will learn to read in spite of poor teaching. On the other side of the spectrum are the boys who require organized, systematic, efficient instruction by a highly qualified teacher trained in research-based sequential, multi-sensory instructional approaches to be successful. The chance of these boys finding their way into the classroom of a teacher who is highly trained to teach reading is slim. It is up to you as parents to fill in the instruction gap with a strong knowledge of how children learn to read, which is where Chapter 6 and the strategies we present for parents to use at home come in.

CHAPTER 6

What Parents Can Do at Home to Increase Reading Abilities

Every parent questions his or her son's status relative to his peers. Children follow predictable stages of reading development (Chall, 1983). The typical developmental sequence begins when your son realizes that words are made up of a series of sounds and starts to recognize rhyme. If the sequence develops as expected, preschoolers learn to recognize the letters of the alphabet and the sounds associated with letters. As a point of reference, I am including the expected progression through the stages of reading. As with any developmental sequence, precise ages for mastering these milestones are arbitrary. I present them as a point of reference and a means by which to track your son's progress.

Developmental Reading Stages

Stage 1: Initial Reading or Decoding Stage (Ages 6–7)

At this stage, your son develops understanding that letters and letter combinations represent sounds. He uses this knowledge to blend together the sounds of phonetically consistent words such as "cat" or "hop." Even though your son understands that individual letters represent discrete sounds, he may still find it difficult to segment sounds in an orally presented sound. For example, if you say /cat/, your son may have difficulty segmenting that word into the discrete sounds of /c/ /a/ /t/. In addition, he may also have difficulty blending the individual sounds. Both of these skills are prerequisites for the decoding process. As such, decoding is the process by which a word is broken into individual phonemes and blended back together to create a word. Your son may reach each of these stages at a later-than-typical age. Keep in mind that your child will need to move through each stage at his own pace.

Stage 2: Confirmation, Fluency, Ungluing From Print (Ages 7–8)

As your son begins to develop fluency and additional strategies to gain meaning from print, he is ready to read without sounding everything out. He will begin to recognize whole words by their visual appearance and letter sequence (orthographic knowledge). He will start recognizing familiar patterns and hopefully reach automaticity in word recognition.

Your son will need extra repetitions to develop the strategies that lead to fluency. Because your son's ability to recognize whole words may be hampered by auditory or visual perceptual problems, as many as 1,000 repetitions may be necessary for mastery of decoding to occur. This is a daunting number. It requires creativity and patience on everyone's part to persevere through this process.

Without commitment to this lengthy and intense process, your son will begin to fall seriously behind. Do not expect the classroom instruction to incorporate this level of intervention, as the skills your son needs are often not explicitly taught and certainly not extensively practiced.

Stage 3: Reading to Learn (Ages 8–14)

Readers in this stage have mastered the "code" and can easily sound out unfamiliar words and read with fluency. Now they must use reading as a tool for acquiring new knowledge. At this stage, word meaning, prior knowledge, and strategic knowledge become more important.

Your child will need help to develop the ability to understand sentences, paragraphs, and chapters as he reads. Reading instruction should include study of word morphology, roots, and prefixes, as well as a number of strategies to aid comprehension. About 40% of children with reading difficulties have problems that are not apparent until they reach fourth grade.

Stage 4: Multiple Viewpoints (Ages 14–18)

In contrast to the previous stage of reading for specific information, students are now exposed to multiple viewpoints about subjects. They are able to analyze what they read, deal with layers of facts and concepts, and react critically to the different viewpoints they encounter.

When your son reaches the phase where reading involves more complex thinking and analysis, he is ready to shine. He may still have difficulty with some of the mechanics of reading, but his mind is well suited to sharing and manipulation of ideas. He will be well prepared to move on to the final, fifth stage of reading—college level and beyond. If you can successfully guide your son through the early stage barriers to this phase, he will be able to excel at understanding and integrating advanced reading material.

The checklist in Figure 6.1 can be used as a guide as you work with your son at home. The checklist is not sequential in nature. Many of

Emerging Reader

	Engages briefly with books shared one-on-one
	Relies on others to read or share books
	Begins to recognize some letters
	Recognizes first name
	Recognizes last name
	Enjoys having books read to him
	Enjoys looking at books on his own
	Repeats words or phrases from familiar books
	Makes up own story with books
	Identifies some letters
	Identifies most letters
	Has an awareness of environmental print (signs, logos, cereal boxes)
	Responds to books read to him
	Begins to choose books on his own
	Retells a story by looking at pictures after repeated listening experiences
	Knows how a book progresses from beginning to end
	Knows the difference between a letter and a word
	Identifies all the letters
	Begins to hear consonant sounds

Early Reader

	Engages in reading reenactment
	Memorizes some texts
	Shows directionality by running finger along lines of text (left to right and top to bottom)
	Reproduces consonant sounds
	Uses initial consonants to identify words
	Begins to remember a few high-frequency sight words
	Matches print words with spoken words in new text
	Rereads familiar stories
	Reads self-created written messages

Figure 6.1. *Checklists for gauging emerging, early, and developing reading skills.*

Early Reader, Continued.

	Retells a familiar story without the book
	Uses pictures as cues when reading text
	Predicts story events, words, and story endings
	Needs encouragement when reading new words or books
	Uses both initial and final consonants to identify words
	Knows what vowels are
	Reads using one-to-one correspondence and self-corrects errors
	Begins to develop fluency with familiar books
	Needs help to select appropriate reading material
	Builds on his high-frequency sight word vocabulary
	Uses beginning, middle, and ending consonants to identify words

Developing Reader

	Discusses and retells story to demonstrate understanding
	Compares or contrasts own experience with story
	Makes connections with other literature
	Reads new text one word at a time but shows some evidence of phrasing
	Corrects most errors that interfere with meaning
	Uses a variety of strategies when reading
	Comments on character, plot, and setting when prompted
	Chooses new as well as previously read books. Begins to analyze words and make connections between:
	Word family patterns
	Small words within a larger word
	Blends
	Consonant digraphs (sh, ch, th, wh, ph)
	Short vowels
	Long vowels
	Silent e
	Y as a vowel
	Digraphs (ai, ay, ea, ee, ei)

Figure 6.1. *Continued.*

61

Developing Reader, Continued.

	Diphthongs (au, oi, oy, oo)
	Prefixes/suffixes
	Compound words
	Contractions
Recognizes high-frequency sight words (approximately 50)	
Is moving toward independence	
Reads fluently with expression most of the time	
Recognizes which errors are important to self-correct	
Demonstrates comprehension of reading material through discussion and retelling	
Changes expression and inflection when reading aloud	
Answers and understands written questions	
Uses prior knowledge to make predictions	
Makes good use of reading time and chooses to read	
Selects appropriate reading material	
Views self as reader	
Retells story including setting, sequence of events, main idea, characters, and conclusion	
Reads fluently with proper expression	
Rarely makes mistakes	
Demonstrates higher levels of thinking skills in comprehension of reading material	
Picks up on nuances in books (humor, sadness, injustice, etc.)	
Makes informed predictions using prior knowledge	
Makes connections independently	
Chooses to read for a variety of purposes	
Welcomes challenges as a reader	
Reads a variety of reading material (fiction, nonfiction, poetry, etc.)	

Figure 6.1. *Continued.*

these skills will occur simultaneously. Use the checklist as a guidepost for instruction, as well as an assessment of where your son is currently located in the reading continuum.

Essential Components of Reading

Your ability to work with your son and help him practice specific reading components can dramatically improve his ability to read. Research shows that there are essential components of reading that must be taught in order to learn to read. You can help you son learn to be a good reader by systematically practicing these components:

> *Alphabetic principle* is made up of two parts: alphabetic under-standing, or the knowledge that words are made up of letters that represent different sounds, and phonological recoding, or using the relation between those letters and sounds to pro-nounce and spell words (National Institute of Child Health and Human Development [NICHD], 2000).

> *Concepts of print* refers to the fundamental principles about reading a book. This includes the basics of how to hold a book to the more abstract concept of "word." The finale occurs with the realization that we combined words into sentences to communicate a message.

> Recognizing and using individual sounds to create words, or *phonemic awareness*. Your son needs to be taught to hear sounds in words and that words are made up of the smallest parts of sound, or phonemes.

> Understanding the relationships between written letters and spoken sounds, or *phonics*. Your son needs to be taught the sounds individual printed letters and groups of letters make. Knowing the relationships between letters and sounds helps children to recognize familiar words accurately and automati-cally and to decode new words.

> Developing the ability to read a text accurately and quickly, or *reading fluency*. Your son must learn to read words rapidly and accurately in order to understand what is read. When

fluent readers read silently, they recognize words automatically. When fluent readers read aloud, they read effortlessly and with expression. Readers who are weak in fluency read slowly, word by word, focusing on decoding words instead of comprehending meaning.

➤ Learning the meaning and pronunciation of words, or *vocabulary development*. Your son needs to actively build and expand his knowledge of written and spoken words, what they mean and how they are used.

➤ Acquiring strategies to understand, remember, and communicate what is read, or *reading comprehension strategies*. Your son needs to be taught comprehension strategies, or the steps good readers use to make sure they understand text. Those who are in control of their own reading comprehension become purposeful, active readers.

Alphabetic Principle

The alphabetic principle can be a challenge to many young readers (Snow et al., 1998). The alphabetic principle is made up of two parts: alphabetic understanding, or the knowledge that words are made up of letters that represent different sounds, and phonological recoding, or using the relation between those letters and sounds to pronounce and spell words (NICHD, 2000). The primary difference between good and poor readers is the ability to use letter-sound correspondence to identify words (Juel & Minden-Cupp, 2004). The combination of instruction in phonemic awareness and letter-sound relationships results in your son's ability to acquire and apply the alphabetic principle early in his reading career, becoming an efficient reader.

Unfortunately, many young children struggle to consistently and automatically identify letters of the alphabet by sight or make the connection between a letter, its name, and its sound. Children who have difficulty making this initial connection often develop difficulties reading words in isolation and in context. They experience a breakdown in developing the alphabetic principle—the letter-sound correspondences and spelling patterns—and in learning how to apply this knowledge in their reading (NICHD, 2000). There are several reasons for this breakdown, including the number of associations that beginning readers must learn:

➢ There are 40 sounds for 52 arbitrary symbols, as well as sounds formed by the combination of these arbitrary symbols (Ehri & McCormick, 2004).

➢ The English language uses a system in which the associations between letters and sounds are totally arbitrary, as there is nothing inherent in the visual symbol that suggests its name or sound.

➢ Several of the letters in the alphabet look alike, which can be confusing.

➢ Letters challenge the unimportance of spatial orientation. A cup is a cup no matter which way it is turned; however, the letter d can become the letter b, p, or q depending on how it is turned.

Teachers typically use their experience, commercial programs and materials, and free interactive websites (e.g., http://www.starfall.com) as interventions. Common activities include alphabet books, games, or forming letters out of clay or Wikki Stix.

Another method for mastering the alphabetic principle is by using integrated picture mnemonics. This involves building a familiar picture around the letter shape. For example, the letter b can be represented through the picture of a bat and baseball so that the picture name begins with the target sound. Research has suggested that prereaders who were taught letter-sound associations through integrated picture mnemonics learned more letter-sound associations than did their peers who were not exposed to the mnemonics. Cardinal Concepts in Education has created an integrated alphabet with accompanying materials that can be purchased at its website (http://www.thecardinalconcepts.com).

Alphabetic Principle Activities

The following are some interactive activities parents can use to help their sons learn alphabetic principles.

➤ Fill an empty cookie sheet with flour or rice and let them trace letters with their fingers. Shake the tin to start over.

➤ Fill a large resealable see-through bag with shaving foam. Close it tight (!) and let your son use his finger to make letters in the foam.

➤ Choose a Letter of the Day or Week. Print out your chosen letter and color it in. Pin it up on a large piece of paper and as your child comes across items, he should write them under the letter or cut out pictures and glue them underneath the letter. You could also turn this into a placemat by laminating the paper.

➤ Teach the letter names by singing the alphabet song. Point to the letters on an alphabet chart as you sing so that your son can see that the letter names match the printed letters.

➤ Make an alphabet book. Give each page a letter of the alphabet, and stick in magazine pictures that begin with the associated letter sound. Let your child read the book with you.

➤ Make alphabet placemats. Cut out lots of letters from magazines and glue them onto to some cardstock. Laminate and use at meal times so your son is frequently exposed to the alphabet.

➤ Make alphabet bookmarks. Write or print the first letter of your child's name onto the top of a blank bookmark. Have him cut out examples of this letter in different fonts from magazines or a picture that begins with this initial letter and glue them onto a bookmark. Use it with your child's favorite books.

➤ Make alphabet popsicle sticks. Buy 26 popsicle sticks and 26 wood cutouts, such as stars or trucks, that you can glue onto the sticks. With a black marker pen, mark each cutout with a letter of the alphabet. Ellen made these and played all sorts of games with them. For example, each day the child (or you) can pick a star to be the letter of the day—then go on a letter hunt around your home to find the letter.

➤ Make or purchase a wall hanging with 26 pockets. Mark each pocket with a letter of the alphabet and put items inside that start with the same letter. (Check out teacher supply stores for ready-made wall hangings.)

➤ Make an alphabet sticker book using purchased stickers. You can get some great ones from craft stores.

➤ Have your son trace his name. Write his name clearly with a black marker on white paper. Tape tracing paper over the paper (this stops the paper from slipping) and let him trace his name with a pencil. This helps him associate the shape of the letters with the letters of his name and is also excellent for those early printing skills. Move on to tracing the rest of the alphabet letters. You could also have your son trace out words he wants to learn, like other family members' or pets' names.

➤ Buy alphabet beads and have your son make his own A–Z bead snake with beads threaded onto a string. Teach the alphabet song and point to each bead as you sing.

➤ Stencil the alphabet around your son's bedroom or onto a piece of furniture or lampshade for his room.

➤ Make tactile letters—use glue to stencil letters onto paper or cardboard and cover them with sand or glitter.

➤ Use alphabet rubber stamps to make decorative cards or bookmarks.

➤ Make some alphabet cookies using letter-shaped cookie cutters, or use the cookie cutters with playdough.

Remember, work for short stretches at a time, as you don't want to frustrate your son. Just spend 10–20 minutes each day on the alphabetic principle, and you'll be amazed by his progress.

Apps for Alphabetic Principle

- *Alphabetic.* This is a challenging letter search game, most suitable for slightly older children due to its settings/features and frantic pace.
- *Alpha Writer.* This is an app for children that teaches learning to read by forming words. This app is good for teaching spelling with phonetics because it reinforces letter sounds, especially when they're combined.
- *Dr. Seuss's ABC.* This app is pricey, but one of the all-time best alphabet apps. It not only emphasizes letters, but also vocabulary, spelling, and picture-word matching.
- *iWriteWords.* This is a fun app, but more focused on writing the alphabet and numbers than learning to recognize them (related but different skills). If kids like "connect the dots"-style tracing, they'll enjoy this one.
- *Super Why!* This app is from PBS, so you know it's fun and based on educational research. The app has four games within it, so there's good value for your money.

Concepts of Print

Concepts of print (also called print concepts) refers to the fundamental principles of reading a book. This includes the basics of how to hold a book to the more abstract concept of what makes a word. The teaching of this concept ends with the realization that we combined words into sentences to communicate a message.

A child needs to know how to hold a book and where to start reading. A child must track words left to right and then continue from the end of one line to the beginning of the next line (return sweep). Although these print concepts are obvious to parents, they are not always obvious for your son. He will easily grasp these concepts if you read to him every day. Fill your home with books, magazines, and newspapers. This encourages the development of both print concepts and awareness.

Print Concepts Activities

The following are examples of easy and free activities that build the concepts of print:

➢ Visit a local library or used bookstore and show your son how to pick up and look at books. Show him how to find the title of a book and, if he's ready, where a description of the book might be located (on the jacket or back).

➢ Write your son's name on his possessions.

➢ Point out environmental print such as stop signs, store names, and street signs.

➢ Let your son catch you enjoying a good book.

➢ As you read to him, let him hold the book and show him where the story starts and ends.

➢ Let your son turn the pages and trace the sentences with his finger as you read.

You can also employ the following specific activities with your child:

➢ *Silly reader.* Hold your son's favorite book upside down and ask questions such as "Is this the correct way to hold a book? How do you hold a book?" Using your finger to trace the sentences, read right to left and then ask questions like "Is that backward? How do I read the lines?" Interpret the illustrations instead of reading the words and then ask questions such as "Should I be reading the pictures or do I read the words?" Start at the back of the book, with the last word, and begin reading backward, asking more questions.

➢ *Print concepts assessment.* Using the same favorite book, give the following directions and note your child's difficulties.
  - Show me the cover (front) of the book.
  - Show me the back of the book.
  - Point to where I start to read.
  - Show me which direction I should read each line.
  - Point to a word. Point to each word as I read it.
  - Point to a letter.

- Count the words.
- Count the letters.
- Show me the spaces between word.
- Show me a period, question mark, or comma.

Apps for Print Concepts

- *Alphabytes.* This is an educational app that helps kids learn their letters, the sounds letters make, how to write both upper- and lowercase letters, and how to spell a few words.

- *The Electric Company Wordball!* This app incorporates video from the popular television show with a game to teach reading and spelling. Kids can listen to some of their favorite music artists as they maneuver through the game.

- *Interactive Alphabet.* This app offers alphabet matching for babies, toddlers, and preschoolers. Your son can hear words, letters, and phonics sounds. It auto advances every 15 seconds.

- *Word Wizard.* This is the first educational app that utilizes natural sounding text-to-speech voices to help kids learn word building and spelling. The Movable Alphabet feature helps kids hear the text they wrote, as well as verify spelling using the built-in spell checker.

Phonemic Awareness

Phonemes are the smallest units composing spoken language. For example, the words "it" and "the" each consist of two sounds or phonemes. Phonemes are different from letters that represent phonemes in the spellings of words. Instruction in phonemic awareness involves teaching children to focus on and manipulate phonemes in spoken syllables and words.

The National Reading Panel (NICHD, 2000) reported that phonemic awareness and letter knowledge are the two best predictors of how well children will learn to read. Phonemic awareness provides foundational knowledge in the alphabetic system and is the ability to notice, think about, and work with the individual sounds in spoken words. An example of phonemic awareness is blending and segmenting the separate sounds of a word. For example, when segmenting the sounds of a word, begin by introducing the word orally. You say "cat." Ask your son to repeat the word. He says "cat." Explain that you would like him to break the word into separate sounds. Place three coins on the table and model segmenting by moving a coin while saying each sound in the word. For blending, separate the three coins on the table. Select a new three-letter word and isolate each sound while touching a coin. Move the coins closer and say each sound in sequence, increasing your speed as you move the coins closer and closer together until your son can successfully blend the word.

Although phonemic awareness is a widely used term in reading, it is often misunderstood. One misunderstanding is that phonemic awareness and phonics are the same thing. Phonemic awareness is the understanding that the sounds of spoken language work together to make words. Phonics is the understanding that there is a relationship between letters and sounds through written language. If boys are to benefit from phonics instruction, they need phonemic awareness. This is because boys who cannot hear and work with the phonemes of spoken words will have a difficult time learning how to relate these phonemes to letters when they see them in written words. Make the activities listed below fun and exciting. Play with sounds. Exaggerate the sounds and emphasize sounds in different positions; initial position (/t/ in take) is easiest, then final position (/l/ in bill), with medial position (/i/ in hit) being the hardest.

Phonemic Awareness Activities

Using Elkonin sound boxes. One technique employed to build phonemic awareness is Elkonin boxes. These are three or more adjacent boxes drawn on paper or white board. To get started using these boxes, do the following:

> ➤ Have your son draw three boxes on a sheet of paper or dry erase board.

➤ Distribute counters to your son (counters can be any single object like small cards, coins, or bean bags). Have him place counters above the boxes. Model the activities before he begins.

➤ Say a three-letter word. For each phoneme, your son moves a counter to each box in a left-to-right progression.

➤ For example, you tell him, "Say the word let." He moves the counters to represent the sounds he hears in the word: /l/ /e/ /t/. He says the word again, sliding him finger below the boxes from left to right.

Other activities for Elkonin boxes include the following:

➤ Ask your son to listen for a certain sound in a word. You should then say a word that has that sound. Your son places a counter in the first box if he hears the sound in the beginning of the word, in the middle box if he hears the sound in the middle of the word, and in the last box if he hears it at the end of the word. For example, "Listen for the /m/ sound in the following words. Place a counter in the first box if you hear the /m/ sound at the beginning of the word; place a counter in the middle box if you hear the sound in the middle of the word; or place it in the last box if you hear the /m/ sound at the end of the word. Listen carefully. The word is ham."

➤ Replace the counters with several letters after appropriate letter-sound correspondences have been introduced. Take the letters a, l, p, s, and n, and have your son place or write the corresponding letters in the boxes for the phonemes as you say words. For example, say, "Lap. The cat sat in my lap." Letter magnets or flash cards could also work well here.

➤ Have your son write letters in the boxes as you dictate words (Blachman, Ball, Black, & Tangle, 2000). For example, say, "Spell the word big. The big dog barked at the squirrel. Big: /b/ /i/ /g/."

➤ Make colored circles or use colored blocks. Have dry erase pens and a predetermined word list available to read to your son. For example, you could pronounce each of the following words one at a time: hat, pet, sit, fish, chip, dot, cup. Ask your son to repeat each word. Have him count the number of phonemes in the word, not necessarily the number of letters, by tapping or clapping each sound. For fish, tap /f/, /i/, /sh/. Direct your son to slide one colored circle or colored block in each cell of the Elkonin box diagram as he repeats the word. For example, fish has three phonemes and will use three boxes. He will say /f/, /i/, /sh/ as he slides the circles into each box.

Sequences of sounds. Collect objects that make interesting and distinctive sounds. Some examples follow. Ask your son to cover his eyes with his hands while you make a familiar noise such as closing the door, sneezing, or playing a key on the piano. By listening carefully and without peeking, he is to try to identify the noise. Once he understands the game, try two noises, one after the other. He will then identify the two sounds in sequence. Add the number of sounds in the sequence until memory load is exhausted. Some noises you might use include:

➤ blowing a whistle,
➤ clapping,
➤ coughing,
➤ crumpling paper,
➤ drumming with fingers,
➤ hammering,
➤ ringing a bell,
➤ sharpening a pencil,
➤ slamming a book,
➤ snapping fingers,
➤ tearing paper, or
➤ whistling.

Name the nonsense. Recite or read aloud a familiar text, changing its words or wording. Your son should raise his hand whenever changes occur. You can change phonemes, words, grammar, and meaning. In addition, you can swap word order, word parts, and order of events. Here are some examples of the "nonsense" that can be created within familiar phrases and rhymes:

> ➤ Once a time upon . . . (reversed words)
> ➤ The little red caboose always came first . . . (substitute words)
> ➤ Twinkle, twinkle little car . . . (substitute words)

Clapping names. When you first introduce this activity, model it by using several names of contrasting lengths. Pronounce the first names of family members syllable by syllable while clapping them out. Then ask your son to say and clap the name along with you. Explain that each clap represents a syllable or word part. After each name has been clapped, ask him, "How many syllables did you hear?" If he has difficulty counting syllables, have him hold two fingers horizontally under his chin, so he can feel his chin drop for each syllable. Placing his hand on his throat will allow your son to feel the vibration of each syllable.

Initial phoneme sort. Create picture cards using magazines or computer clip art. Paste the pictures on index cards and laminate if possible. Spread selected pictures in front of your son. Then ask him to find the picture whose name starts with a selected initial phoneme.

As each picture is found, he will name the picture and the initial phoneme. For example, you can ask: "What picture begins with the sound /r/?" He might respond: "Ruler. /r/."

Initial phoneme sort advanced. Group the phonemes into sets of three. Collect multiple picture cards for the three distinct phonemes. For example, start with the phonemes /t/, /m/, and /f/. Group phonemes that are easily distinguishable. Avoid grouping phonemes such as /v/ and /f/ or /b/ and /p/ because of their sound and formation similarities. As your son becomes more competent in distinguishing speech sounds, you may then begin to incorporate more challenging groupings. Place the picture cards in front of your son. He will then sort them based on their common initial consonant sound. If three phonemes prove to be too difficult, adjust the cards to represent two initial phonemes.

Phoneme substitution. In this oral activity, your son will make new words by replacing the first sound in the word with the target sound. For example, target the phoneme /s/. Ask your son to sub-stitute the /h/ in "hand" with /s/. He should respond with "sand." Some additional words to use with the targeted /s/ phoneme are: "hit," "well," "funny," "bun," "mad," "bend," and "rat." With the substitution of /s/ in the initial position, the words become "sit," "sell," "sunny," "sad," "send," and "sat."

Secret code. This is a technique for building phonemic aware-ness in which your son listens to a sequence of separately spoken pho-nemes (e.g., /b/ /a/ /t/), then combines them to form a single word ("bat"). You will need picture cards with pictures of words contain-ing three or four sounds. Blending sounds is the process of smoothly joining phonemes to come up with a pronunciation close enough to a word to access the word. A simple blending activity is Secret Code, a guessing game. Turn a picture card face down and name its phonemes (e.g., /h/ /a/ /t/). When your son blends the phonemes and guesses the word, you show him the picture. You also have the option of bring-ing out the Elkonin boxes. While pointing to each box, your son must repeat the phonemes /h/ /a/ /t/ over and over and faster and faster until he knows the identity of the picture.

What's my secret picture? Place multiple picture cards in a bag or box. Select a picture from the bag. Explain that you have a secret picture, and you will give a hint by saying the sounds that make up the name of your secret. Say, "I will name my secret pictures in sounds and when you figure out what it is, it will be your turn." Pronounce the name of the secret picture phoneme by phoneme. For a picture of a cat, you will say /c/ /a/ /t/. When your son guesses the word "cat," he gets the card. Then he should select a picture and name a secret word for you. In this way he gets practice in blending and segmenting phonemes. Work up from short (two- and three-sound) words to longer ones as your son becomes more adept at hearing the sounds. Examples of secret pictures include the following: ape, bean, book, bow, bread, brick, broom, cheese, desk, dog, and dress.

Phonics—The Relationship Between Written and Spoken Letters and Sounds

The National Reading Panel, composed of experts in the field of literacy, was asked by the United States Congress to determine what the research said about the teaching of phonics. To ensure the soundness of its findings, the National Reading Panel (NICHD, 2000) chose to review only studies that met rigorous criteria for research studies. They concluded that phonics is an essential ingredient in beginning reading instruction and found that:

➢ Systematic and explicit phonics instruction—phonics instruction that is direct and follows a particular sequence—is more effective than phonics instruction that is not systematic or no phonics instruction at all.

➢ Systematic, explicit phonics instruction is most effective when it begins in kindergarten or first grade.

➢ Systematic, explicit phonics instruction improves children's word recognition, spelling, and reading comprehension skills.

➢ Systematic, explicit phonics instruction benefits all children, regardless of their socioeconomic status.

➢ Systematic, explicit phonics instruction most benefits children who are having difficulty learning to read.

Phonics instruction is only one part of a complete reading program for beginning readers. Effective beginning reading programs should also emphasize reading fluency, vocabulary development, and text comprehension. Phonics instruction emphasizes letter-sound relationships and their use in reading (decoding) and spelling (encoding). The primary focus of phonics instruction is to help beginning readers understand how letters are linked to sounds (phonemes) to form letter-sound relationships and spelling patterns and to help them learn how to apply this knowledge in their reading of text.

Types of Phonics Instructional Methods and Approaches

Phonics instruction varies relative to the explicitness by which the phonic elements are taught. Many synthetic phonics approaches use direct instruction in teaching phonics and then provide practice in decodable text formats that focus on the skills being taught. Embedded phonics approaches are typically less explicit and use decodable text for practice less frequently.

Systematic phonics instruction produces significant benefits for students in kindergarten through sixth grade and for children having difficulty learning to read. The ability to read and spell words is enhanced in kindergarteners who received systematic beginning phonics instruction. First graders who are taught phonics systematically are better able to decode and spell, and they showed significant improvement in their ability to comprehend text. Older children receiving phonics instruction are better able to decode and spell words and to read text orally.

Across all grade levels, systematic phonics instruction improved the ability of good readers to spell. The effects of systematic early phonics instruction are significant and substantial in kindergarten and first grade, indicating that systematic phonics instruction should be implemented at those ages and grade levels. Explicit, systematic phonics instruction is a valuable and essential part of a successful reading program. Remember, it is critical to understand that the prerequisite to phonics instruction is phonemic awareness. Your son needs to be able to blend spoken sounds together and break spoken words into their individual sounds to be successful in phonics instruction.

There are several different types of phonics instructional approaches that vary according to the unit of analysis or how letter-sound combinations are represented to the student.

Analogy phonics. Teaching students unfamiliar words by analogy to known words, or recognizing that the rime segment of an unfamiliar word is identical to that of a familiar word, and then blending the known rime with the new word onset, such as reading *brick* by recognizing that -ick is contained in the known word kick, or reading *stump* by analogy to the word jump).

Analytic phonics. Teaching students to analyze letter-sound relationships in previously learned words to avoid pronouncing sounds in isolation.

Embedded phonics. Teaching students phonics skills by embedding phonics instruction in text reading. This is a more implicit approach that relies to some extent on incidental learning.

Phonics through spelling. This technique involves teaching students to segment words into phonemes and to select letters for those phonemes (i.e., teaching students to spell words phonemically).

Synthetic phonics. Teaching students explicitly to convert letters into sounds (phonemes) and then blend the sounds to form recognizable words.

Phonics Terminology

To understand written material about phonics, parents should be familiar with the following terms: vowels, consonants, consonant blends (or clusters), consonant digraphs, vowel digraphs, and diphthongs. Each of these is explained below in detail, as well as more briefly in Appendix B: Glossary of Reading Terms.

Vowels. The letters a, e, i, o, and u represent vowel sounds, and the letters w and y take on the characteristics of vowels when they appear in the final position in a word or syllable. The letter y also has the characteristics of a vowel in the medial (middle) position in a word or syllable.

Consonants. Letters other than vowels generally represent consonant sounds. W and y have the characteristics of consonants when they appear in the initial position in a word or syllable.

Consonant blends (or clusters). Two or more adjacent consonant letters whose sounds are blended together, with each individual sound retaining its identity, constitute a consonant blend. Consonant blends (also called consonant clusters) are groups of two or three consonants in words that each make a distinct consonant sound, such as /bl/ or /spl/. Consonant blends include:

/bl/	/gl/	/sn/
/br/	/gr/	/sp/
/cl/	/pr/	/st/
/cr/	/sc/	/sw/
/dr/	/sk/	/tr/
/fl/	/sl/	/tw/
/fr/	/sm/	

Some three-letter consonant blends are:

/nth/	/shr/	/squ/
/sch/	/spl/	/str/
/scr/	/spr/	

For example, although the first three sounds in the word strike are blended smoothly, listeners can detect the separate sounds of /s/, /t/, and /r/ being produced in rapid succession. Other examples are the /spl/ in splash, the /fr/ in frame, the /cl/ in click, and the /br/ in bread, to mention a few. Many teaching materials refer to these letter combinations as consonant clusters rather than consonant blends. The Enchanted Learning site (http://www.enchantedlearning.com/consonantblends) has examples of words beginning with consonant blends, as well as many great activities and worksheets.

Consonant digraphs. Two adjacent consonant letters that represent a single speech sound constitute a consonant digraph. For example, /sh/ is a consonant digraph in the word shore because it represents one sound and not a blend of the sounds of s and h. Other consonant digraphs include:

/ch/	/ph/	/wh/
/gh/	/sh/	/wr/
/kn/	/tch/	
/ng/	/th/	

Vowel digraphs. Two adjacent vowel letters that represent a single speech sound constitute a vowel digraph. In the word foot, /oo/ is a vowel digraph.

Diphthongs. Vowel sounds that are so closely blended that they can be treated as single vowel units for the purposes of word identification are called *diphthongs*. When creating a diphthong sound, one has to move the mouth from one position to another. For example, when making the /ow/ sound, the person begins by opening the mouth wide and then changing it to a small circle. Although not all diphthongs require a change of mouth position, most do.

These sounds are actually vowel blends, because the vocal mechanism produces two sounds instead of one. Diphthongs include:

/aw/	/ou/	/oi/
/au/	/ow/	/oy/

Multisensory Teaching Methods

Samuel T. Orton pioneered the study of learning disabilities. He is best known for his work examining the causes and methods of treatment for dyslexia, including The Orton-Gillingham method. Orton's (1919) study of reading difficulties in children led him to hypothesize that "these individuals have failed to establish appropriate cerebral organization to support the association of visual words with their spoken forms" (p. 286).

The Orton-Gillingham method is the grandfather of structured, sequential, multisensory teaching of written language. It is based upon the use of association as to how a letter or word looks, how it sounds, and how the speech organs feel when producing it. Also incorporated are the common rules of the English language. Older students are challenged to learn syllable patterns, common prefixes and suffixes, and Latin and Greek word parts. (See http://www.orton-gillingham. com for more information.) The Orton-Gillingham method has spawned many variations many for teaching phonics. These include the Slingerland Approach, The Spalding Method, Project Read, Alphabetic Phonics, The Herman Method, and the Wilson Reading System. In addition, other approaches incorporate aspects of Orton's work. Examples of the modified approaches are the Sequential English Education and Starting Over.

Two additional well-known intervention models are the Association Method and the Lindamood-Bell methods. Both of these are based on research that has involved hearing- and language-impaired individuals. We will take a look at each method, keeping in mind that to implement any of these methods you have two choices. First, you can use the contact information to find a trained tutor in your area. Second, you can decide to be trained yourself. Each organization has its own requirements for becoming certified. Often, an internship is involved. Materials can be purchased with or without training. Being trained yourself will involve a large initial investment and a great deal of commitment, but will save you much money in the long run.

> ➤ *Alphabetic Phonics.* This methodology evolved directly from Orton-Gillingham and combines the auditory learning modality for spelling, the visual modality for reading, and the kinesthetic modality for handwriting. Materials include The Instant Spelling Deck (used for a daily 3-minute drill that focuses on the most probable spelling of each of the 44 speech sounds) and the Initial Reading Deck (a set of 98 cards with picture key words that are chosen by students and are used to teach each of the 44 speech sounds). Assessments provide a record of students' progress in reading, spelling, handwriting, and alphabetizing. For more information, contact School Specialty at 800-225-5750 or visit the store online at http://www.eps.schoolspecialty.com.

> ➤ *The Association Method.* The Association Method incorporates multisensory teaching, the teaching of sound/symbol relationships for reading, and the use of cursive writing for initial instruction. Children still learn to read manuscript type, but write only in cursive. Unique to this method is that a slower temporal rate of speech is used to provide children more time to process words and more time to observe the speaker's lip movements. Precise articulation is required from the beginning. Colors are used to differentiate phonemes within words and to highlight verbs and new concepts in language structures. An individual notebook is created for each child to document what has been learned. For more information, contact

the DuBard School for Language Disorders at the University of Southern Mississippi at 601-266-5223 or visit the center's website at http://www.usm.edu/dubard.

➤ *The Herman Method.* This sequence of instruction starts each student at his point of deficit and sequentially teaches him mastery of each skill level. Expansion of each skill occurs vertically and horizontally as in an inverted pyramid. A combination of visual, auditory, kinesthetic, and tactile stimuli help each child compensate for visual and auditory processing problems. All exercises are carefully sequenced and each activity is repeated until automaticity is reached. The Herman Method provides support in decoding and encoding skills, sight word recognition, structural analysis, use of contextual clues, dictionary skills, and comprehension skills. For more information or to purchase materials, visit http://www.soprislearning.com/cs/Satellite/New_Herman_Method_Overview?cmsid=Sopris.

➤ *Lindamood-Bell methods.* One of the Lindamood-Bell methods is The Lindamood® Phonemic Sequencing program (LiPS). LiPS is designed to stimulate phonemic awareness. Children focus on the mouth actions that produce speech sounds. They use this awareness to verify sounds within words. This allows them to become self-correcting in reading, spelling, and speech. Another methodology is The Visualizing and Verbalizing for Language Comprehension and Thinking program (V/V). The V/V program develops concept imagery through a precise series of steps that begin with expressive language and then extend from a word to paragraphs with images. For more information, contact Lindamood-Bell Learning Processes at 800-233-1819 or visit the store online at http://www.lindamoodbell.com.

➤ *Project Read.* Project Read provides an alternative approach to teaching reading and written expression concepts and skills in mainstream classrooms as well as in special education. In its initial form, Project Read was limited to being a decoding/encoding program. As it became apparent that students had more pervasive language learning problems, the program was expanded to include reading comprehension and written expression. For more information, contact Language Circle Enterprises and Project Read at 800-450-0343 or visit the company's website at http://www.projectread.com.

> *Sequential English Education.* The Sequential English Education (SEE) program is a multisensory structured language approach to teaching reading, writing, and spelling for struggling readers. The initial phase emphasizes the mastery of the code of the English language as well as the alphabetic and phonetic system. It is age-appropriate for 5- and 6-year-old children, and instruction should be one-on-one or in small groups of no more than seven students. The SEE program uses a textured memory board for a visual-auditory-tactile-kinesthetic input of new material. Comprehension skills are sequential and begin with word meanings and progress to sentence paraphrasing. For more information, contact The Sequential English Education Training Program at The June Shelton School and Evaluation Center at 972-774-1772 or visit the school's website at http://www.shelton.org.

> *The Slingerland Approach.* The Slingerland Approach was developed for preventive instruction. Today it is used both as a preventive and remedial approach. Delivery of the method can occur in classrooms, in small groups, and in one-to-one settings. It is appropriate for students ranging from primary grade to adults. Oral expression, decoding, reading comprehension, spelling, handwriting, and written expression are all taught with the integrated direct instructional approach. Guided practice of these skills supports the goal of independent reading and written expression. For more information, contact the Slingerland Institute for Literacy at 425-453-1190 or visit the organization's website at http://www.slingerland.org.

> *The Spalding Method.* This method is delivered as integrated, multisensory instruction in listening, speaking, writing, spelling, and reading. The Spalding principles guide lesson plans, instruction, and decisions. These principles assert that learn-

ing should be child-centered and multisensory. In addition, learning should encourage higher level thinking, produce quality work, recognize the value and importance of tasks, and integrate language arts into all curriculum areas. For more information, contact Spalding Education International at 623-434-1204 or visit the organization's website at http://www.spalding.org.

➤ *Starting Over.* This instructional approach is multifaceted in that it includes diagnosis and remediation of decoding, spelling, vocabulary, writing, handwriting, and reading comprehension. The program is based on the belief that children and adults with dyslexia can learn to read, spell, and write if they are diagnosed and taught using a multisensory, structured language approach. In addition, teachers can be taught to do both the diagnosis and the remediation. Most significant is the belief that individuals with dyslexia can be taught to overcome their difficulty in distinguishing the differences among sounds, thus leading to the capacity to easily decode text and then ultimately move to comprehension. For more information, contact Starting Over at 212-769-2760 or visit the website at http://www.knighteducation.com.

➤ *The Wilson Reading System.* The Wilson Reading System is a 12-step remedial reading and writing program for individuals with a language-based learning disability. This program is based on the Orton-Gillingham philosophy and principles and current phonological coding research. The power of this method rests in the fact that it teaches the structure of words so that students master the coding system for reading and spelling. The language system is presented in a simple, systematic, and cumulative manner. This makes it manageable for a young child as well as an adult. Visualization techniques are used for comprehension. For more information, contact Wilson Language Training at 800-899-8454 or visit the company's website at http://www.wilsonlanguage.com.

Vowels	CVC Words
/a/	bat, cat, tag
/e/	get, den, hem
/i/	hit, lip, pin
/o/	hop, dog, top
/u/	bug, hut, sun

Figure 6.2. *CVC words.*

Phonics Rules and Activities

There are six syllable types. It is very helpful for struggling readers to be able to identify the syllable types in words when trying to read or spell. The sound a vowel makes often depends upon what type of syllable it is in. The following pages provide activities for each syllable type that can be implemented at home or suggested to your son's teacher.

CVC rule. If a single vowel is surrounded by consonants, then it usually has a short sound. For example, in the word cat, the vowel /a/ is surrounded by consonants. Ellen often teaches this as the "bully rule." The consonants put the "squeeze" on the vowel, thus forcing it to say its shortened sounds. Figure 6.2 includes a chart of the vowels and sample CVC words.

Word sort for word families. Select three word families and write one CVC word for each. Let's begin with the word families /it/, /ip/, and /ill/. Next, write "will," "sit," and "zip" on index cards. These will be your anchor words. Put these anchor words on the table. Make 10 additional word cards for each word family.

Demonstrate how to isolate each sound by tapping it on your arm. If the child is right handed, the first sound is tapped on the left shoulder, the middle sound is tapped on the left elbow, and the final sound is tapped on the left wrist. If the child is left handed, the first sound is tapped on the right wrist, the middle sound is tapped on the right elbow, and the final sound is tapped on the right shoulder. This maintains the left to right tracking of text. After demonstrating the technique, have your son model the tapping procedure with the anchor words for each word family. Go to your additional word card stack and pick up another word. Model the tapping procedure, then ask your son to place the card under the appropriate header. You may need to repeat the tapping of the header words. Once all words are sorted, have your son read all of the words using the tapping technique as needed. After doing this sort with your son, use other common word families to create more sorts. Each sort should be kept in a zipper bag and labeled with the sort criteria. Keep these available for independent work.

CVCe rule. This pattern is often described as the "magical e" rule. If the e is at the end of a word, it signals to the reader that the preceding vowel says its alphabet name or long sound. When a one-syllable word has an e at the end and a vowel in the middle, the first vowel is usually long and the e is silent. In working with students, Ellen continues the bully metaphor, describing the silent e at the end of the CVCe word as the strong silent hero who makes the consonant bullies release their hold on the vowel, allowing the vowel to say its alphabet name or long vowel sound. Create a stack of word cards with the following header words as your guide: make, male, pane. These word cards will be used in the following activities:

➢ *Regular sort.* This is your son's opportunity to begin exploring and categorizing the words in his sort by creating columns or groups of words just as he did with CVC words. Again, use word families to create your own sorts. Follow the same instructional procedures that you did with CVC words.

➢ *Blind sort.* Your son sorts 10–12 words without the header words. He must discover the rule for sorting.

➢ *Speed sort.* Using a stopwatch, your son can see how fast he can correctly sort his words.

➢ *Word hunt.* In this sort, select a magazine or newspaper and search for words that fit into a designated sort.

➢ *PowerPoint fun.* Take the words used in previous sorts and create a PowerPoint file with one word on each slide. Your son will read the word off the slide. Set the slide transition time at 5-second intervals and decrease the time as your son improves. This is great for improving word level fluency and automatic decoding.

Vowel team rule. Your son might be taught the phrase, "When two vowels go walking, the first vowel does the talking." The first vowel says its name (long vowel sound) and the second vowel is silent. This is true with most vowel pairs, but not for diphthongs. Examples of vowel teams include ee, ea, eo, and ai. Diphthong examples include ou, oi, and ow.

Following the bully metaphor again, the first vowel hires a strong silent vowel bodyguard that releases the hold of the bully consonants and allows the first vowel to say its alphabet name or long sound. Diphthongs are not pure vowel teams. They are two-vowel sounds that are so closely blended that they can be treated as a single-vowel unit. These sounds are actually vowel blends, because the vocal mechanism produces two sounds instead of one, as in the case with vowel digraphs. An example of a diphthong is the /ou/ in out.

Draw a man (better known as hangman). Play this game to help your son sharpen his vowel team and diphthong spelling and word-decoding skills.

> ➤ Start the game choosing a word containing the target vowel team or digraph.
> ➤ Place one dash on the bottom of a piece of paper for each letter of the word chosen.
> ➤ Draw a box at the top of the paper for drawing the "man."
> ➤ Have your son guess one letter at a time, or he can use a turn to guess the entire word or words.
> ➤ Fill in the letter (everywhere it appears) on the appropriate dash (or dashes) each time your son guesses correctly.
> ➤ Add one body part to the drawing each time the letter chosen is not in the word. Begin by drawing a head and then add eyes, ears, nose, hair, body, legs, and arms.
> ➤ If he figures out the word before you have drawn the entire body, he gets a point. Go for 10 points, changing the vowel team or digraph each round.

Make a word square. Draw a square. Divide the square into nine equal parts. Place a vowel team or digraph in the middle box. Place consonants in remaining boxes (see Figure 6.3 for a completed

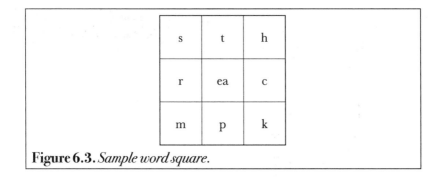

s	t	h
r	ea	c
m	p	k

Figure 6.3. *Sample word square.*

word square). Using the designated vowel team or digraph, see how many words your son can write. Give points for the number of words, the longest words, and the hardest words. Set a point goal each time you play.

R-controlled vowels (also called Bossy R). When the letter r follows a vowel, the vowel is usually forced to change its sound. That's why it is called the "Bossy R." In most small words with one vowel in the middle, that vowel has a short vowel sound, as in the words bad, hen, sit, fox, and fun. The sound of the vowel changes if we replace the last letter of each of these words with the letter r. For example, bat changes to bar, hen to her, sit to sir, fox to for, fun to fur. The sound /ar/ is usually spelled with the letters ar and /or/ is usually spelled or. The sound /er/ can be spelled with the vowels i, e, or u preceding the letter r. The website Word Way Bossy R website (http://www.wordway.us.com/BossyR.htm) provides great examples of the Bossy R in action.

Bossy R concentration. Print two copies of r-controlled vowel word cards, preferably on cardstock, heavy paper, or index cards. Cut out the word cards and select 40 cards (20 pairs). Be sure to include some words from each of the five r-controlled vowel combinations (/ar/, /er/, /ir/, /or/, /ur/).

1. Place the selected cards face down on the table and mix them up.
2. Arrange the face-down cards into rows on the table.
3. You and your son take turns flipping over two cards at a time. While cards are being flipped up, read the words aloud. If a

match is made, keep the pair of cards and take another turn. If another match is made, keep the pair or cards and take another turn. If a match is not made, return the cards face down on the table and it's the other person's turn. See how well you can remember the cards!

4. When all of the cards on the table have been matched, count your pairs. The player with the most pairs wins.

Open syllable. An open syllable ends in a vowel. The vowel has a long vowel sound, as in the first syllable of apron. You want to begin with high-frequency open syllable words such as me, he, he, we, the, and go. Avoid rule exceptions such as to and do at this point. Continue the bully metaphor and explain that the bullies left the back door open so the vowel can say its name.

Open syllable activities. Two activities that can easily be made at home require construction paper and glue. In the first activity, cut out a house and decorate it with your son's help. Cut out an off-center door that can swing open and closed. To the left of the door, paste letters that make an open syllable when the door is open. An example would be to paste the word "go" to the left of the door when the door is open. Behind the open door paste a consonant that will create a closed syllable when the door is closed. For this example use the consonant *t*. With the door open, the word is "go"; with the door closed, the word is "got." Sets of these are fun to make with your son and then put in an area where she can work independently.

A second activity for working with open syllables requires a transparent ruler and a list of two-syllable words containing both open and closed initial syllables. Examples of two-syllable words with an initial open syllable could include rodent, minus, tulip, begin, and station. Examples of two-syllable words with an initial closed syllable could include muffin, helmet, letter, and contact. Take the transparent ruler and place it so it covers the first word. We'll use the word begin as an example. Slide the ruler to the left until the first vowel is uncovered. With our example of begin, the ruler will uncover the syllable "be," leaving "gin" under the ruler but still visible. Ask your son to tap the first syllable, focusing on the fact that it is an open syllable and the e is making its long sound. He then needs to tap the syllable left under the transparent ruler and determine if he has made a real word. In this case he has, so he will draw a line indicating the appropriate syllable division. If he does not create a real word, he then slides the ruler over to the left, revealing the next consonant. With the word muffin, he would determine that the first syllable is not open because a real word is not made. Once the ruler slides over and uncovers the letter f and creates the closed syllable "muf," then a real word is made and he makes the correct syllable division. Continue with the rest of the list.

Consonant (C-le). This syllable is found in words like handle, puzzle, and middle. The e is silent and the consonant + l are pronounced like a blend. Also known as the stable final syllable, consonant-le combinations are found only at the ends of words. If a C-le syllable is combined with an open syllable—as in cable, bugle, or title—there is no doubled consonant. If one is combined with a closed syllable—as in dabble, topple, or little—a double consonant results. Not every consonant is found in a C-le syllable. These are the ones that are used in English:

-ble (bubble)	-kle (wrinkle)	-tle (whittle)
-cle (cycle)	-stle (whistle)	-gle (bugle)
-ckle (trickle)	-fle (rifle)	-sle (hassle)
-dle (riddle)	-ple (quadruple)	-zle (puzzle)

Word sort. This activity is a traditional word sort in which your son is asked to sort words that all have the consonant-le pattern, but some begin with an open syllable and the others begin with a closed syllable. Review these two syllable types before beginning. Words for sort might include those in Figure 6.4. Make and cut out your word cards and provide a header (open or closed) for each category. Provide help as needed.

Divide and conquer. Using the same word list, ask your son to highlight the consonant-le in each word. Once highlighted, he will then separate the highlighted syllable using a slash mark (no/ble). Have him identify the first syllable as open or closed and then pronounce the word.

Closed Syllable	Open Syllable
cattle	fable
hassle	gable
bubble	able
babble	bugle
paddle	rifle
scrabble	idle

Figure 6.4. *Closed and open syllable words for sorting.*

PowerPoint fun. Take the words from the chart and create a PowerPoint file with one word on each slide. Set the slide transition time at 5-second intervals and decrease the time as your son improves. This is great for improving word level fluency and automatic decoding.

Apps for Phonics

- *ABC Phonics Rocks!* ABC Phonics Rocks! teaches students their letter sounds. On the "Letters" section of the game, it displays the alphabet, and when students touch a letter, its sound is produced. On the "Words" section of the game, the student is shown a picture of a simple word to spell, such as hat, and blank spaces are provided for the student to fill in letters to spell the word. When the student touches a space, they hear the phoneme that goes there, and then can choose the corresponding letter to go in that spot. We like that this app says the sounds of the letters rather than their names.

- *ABC PocketPhonics.* ABC PocketPhonics has two games. In the first game, the student is shown a letter, hears its sound, and is then asked to trace the letter. The tracing task models the correct directionality and gives the child feedback about whether he traced the letter correctly or not. In the second game, the narrator says a phoneme and asks the child to pick the corresponding letter. Then the narrator says the next sound in the word until the whole word is spelled. After all of the letters are chosen, the narrator models blending of the new word. Most of the words are simple CVC words with short vowels.

- *Build a Word.* This is a letter-matching game that doesn't teach children how to create words themselves. Build a Word displays a letter on the screen, and then the child must choose the matching letter from a variety of floating letters. The narrator says the letter name, then displays the next letter in the word until the student has matched all of the letters in the word. The student then blends the letters together to make a word. The drawback of this app is that the number of words the child is able to build is very limited.

- *Clifford's BE BIG With Words.* This app is centered on a story: Clifford's friend Jetta is painting and needs ideas for what to paint. Below an art easel, the student can choose from 2–4 capital letters to give Jetta some ideas for words to be painted. The student drags and drops any letter he wants into each slot. The game is designed so there is no chance the child will produce a nonword. Once the three slots are filled, the narrator sounds out each letter and then says, "You spelled _____!" This app is limited by the fact that it says the letter sound instead of the letter name when the student is dragging and dropping each letter onto the easel. However, this app is great reinforcement for students who are learning to spell simple CVC (consonant-vowel-consonant) words with short vowels.

- *Doodle Buddy.* In this app, the student uses his finger to draw on the screen. As he draws, he has options to change the color of the paint and the size of the crayon. Doodle Buddy is a great app for adding a multisensory component to a variety of skill-based lessons. There is an option to save completed pictures into iPhoto, which can then be transferred to your computer, printed, and added to your son's portfolio. This is a great app for reluctant writers who balk at using paper and pencil. This new dynamic is a true motivator.

* *Phonics Made Easy Flash Action.* Phonics Made Easy Flash Action app has been developed to help children sharpen important phonics skills for reading success. In using this app, children will explore beginning and ending letter sounds, recognize long and short vowel sounds, familiarize themselves with rhyming families, and work with letter blends. Audio within the app makes phonic skills much easier to learn because children can hear letter sounds while working.

Fluency

Good readers read quickly, effortlessly, and with automaticity. When a task that formerly required attention for its performance can be performed without attention, the task is being done automatically. Automaticity in information processing, then, simply means that information is processed with little attention. One way to determine if a person is performing a process automatically is to give him two tasks to perform at the same time. If the tasks can be performed simultaneously, at least one of them is being done automatically. When a fluent reader reads aloud, he reads with tone and expression, inserting appropriate pauses and emphasizing appropriate words. If children labor to decode words, then they do not have attention or mental resources left over to dedicate to comprehension and enjoyment.

According to the National Reading Panel (NICHD, 2000), fluency is the ability to read a text quickly, accurately, and with proper expression. If individuals are low in fluency, they also have difficulty with comprehension. The National Reading Panel (NICHD, 2000) found that guided repeated reading procedures are effective in improving reading fluency and overall reading achievement. These procedures improve word recognition, fluency, and comprehension.

Administering Fluency Assessments

Directions. The following are some guidelines for administering fluency assessments:

➤ Give your son a reading passage at his instructional level that he has not seen before.

➤ Fluency assessments are always done as "cold reads"; that is, they are done with material that is new to the person being tested.

➤ Explain that you would like him to read the passage out loud and then answer questions and tell you about the story. Then say, "When you are ready, you may begin."

➤ Start your stopwatch when the student reads the first word.

➤ Follow along on your copy of the passage as the student reads. Place a line through each word that is read incorrectly or omitted.

➤ Place a check above each word that is read correctly.

➤ If your son substitutes or mispronounces a word, put a line through the word and write the word he said above it.

➤ If your son does not correctly say the word within 3 seconds, say the word for him and circle the word to mark it as incorrect. Self-corrections and repetitions are not marked as errors.

➤ At the end of one minute, stop timing and place a bracket after the last word read.

➤ Have your son finish reading the passage.

➤ Ask your son to retell the story.

How to score. Use the following steps to determine your son's fluency rate.

➤ Count the number of words read in one minute.

➤ Count each word you circled or put a line through. The total is the number of errors made. Subtract this number from the number of words read in one minute to arrive at the oral reading fluency rate, or words correct per minute score.

➤ Compare your son's reading rate to the scores at http://www.readinga-z.com/assess/fluency-passage.html. Fluency passages can also be purchased at http://teacher.scholastic.com/products/fluencyformula/assessment.htm.

Scoring the retelling. Score the retelling using the following criteria. Assign an appropriate numeric score from 0 to 5 for future comparison.

> ➤ No recall or minimal recall of only a fact of two from the passage.
>
> ➤ Student recalls a number of unrelated facts of varied importance.
>
> ➤ Student recalls the main idea of the passage with a few supporting details.
>
> ➤ Student recalls the main idea along with supporting details, although not necessarily organized logically or sequentially as presented in the passage.
>
> ➤ Student recalls a comprehensive summary of the passage, presented in a logical order and/or with details, and includes a statement of main idea.
>
> ➤ Student makes reasonable connections beyond the text to his own personal life, another text, or other source.

Activities to Develop Fluency

Repeated readings. The more your son hears or reads a story, the better he comprehends it and the more he will love it (Harvey & Goudvis, 2000). Jay Samuels (1979) has developed an instructional procedure to help students increase their fluency and accuracy through rereading. The steps in the individualized procedure are:

> ➤ Have the students choose a textbook or trade book and read a passage from the book aloud while you record the reading time and any errors.
>
> ➤ Have the student practice rereading the passage orally or silently several times. Then have the student reread the passage and record the reading time.
>
> ➤ Have the student compare his reading time between the first and last readings. Then the student prepares a graph to show his growth between the first and last readings.

Reader's theater. Reader's theater is a dramatic performance of a script by a group of readers (Black & Stave, 2007). It is a reading activity in which readers read stories or plays with expressive voices and use gestures to help the audience visualize the action (Sloyer, 1982). In reader's theater, each student assumes a part, rehearses by reading and rereading his character's lines in the script, and then does a performance of the reading for his classmates or audience. The backbone of reader's theater is repeated reading, a tested and proven method for increasing reading fluency in short-term studies (NICHD, 2000). Classroom-based research has found that the reader's theater approach to fluency instruction leads to significant improvement in reading fluency and overall reading achievement (Morrow & Gambrell, 2011).

There are multiple advantages of using reader's theater with students, including:

➢ The level of difficulty of different parts within a script can vary widely (Worthy & Prater, 2002).

➢ Students have an opportunity to enjoy reading good literature and, by doing this, they engage with text, interpret characters, and bring the text to life (Keehn, Harmon, & Shoho, 2008).

➢ Reader's theater incorporates the principles of effective fluency instruction, such as modeling fluent reading, assisted reading, and repeated reading, within an authentic and purposeful framework (Morrow & Gambrell, 2011).

➢ Reader's theater is a highly motivating and engaging reading activity (Morrow et al., 2011).

To incorporate reader's theater in your son's reading instruction, begin by choosing the right text. You can choose scripts from online, pull them from books of plays, or create your own scripts. Texts for reader's theater are chosen based on the age of the students, the length of the text, and the suitability of the language and plot. The steps for reader's theater include:

1. *Adapt the text.* To adapt a text to reader's theater, choose the selection your son likes as a script, eliminate the parts that are unnecessary, and highlight the characters' names.

2. *Rehearse.* Select a text, then read and discuss it while clarifying the meaning of unfamiliar vocabulary. On the second reading, your son repeats each line in a choral response after you. Discuss how to use his voice, gestures, and facial expressions to interpret the character he is reading. Read the script several times, aiming for accurate pronunciation, voice, and inflections.

3. *Perform.* Reader's theater can be presented on a "stage" or in front of the family. During the performance, readers usually hold the script in their left hand, so that the right hand is free for gestures. If the reader is sitting, he may stand to read his lines. If he is standing, he may step forward to read. The emphasis should be on expressive quality of the reader's voices and intonation.

Your son can create his own reader's theater scripts from stories he has read about or topics that are related to thematic units learned in school (Flynn, 2007). Ask your son to complete a "quick write" in his journal to reflect on what he liked about his reader's theater practice and performance. As a family, you can create backgrounds, costumes, masks, or props. Creating the background and set allows a better understanding of story's setting, purpose, and intended audience. Following the performance, talk about the experience, either as performers or as listeners.

The following are web sources for reader's theater scripts:

➤ http://www.teachingheart.net/readerstheater.htm
➤ http://www.storycart.com
➤ http://www.readinglady.com
➤ http://www.margiepalatini.com
➤ http://www.fictionteachers.com/classroomtheater/theater.html
➤ http://www.literacyconnections.com/testReadersTheater.php
➤ http://www.vtaide.com/png/theatre.htm
➤ http://www.timelessteacherstuff.com

Reader's theater scripts can also be bought commercially from several sources:

- ➢ *Portage and Main Press* (http://www.portageandmainpress.com). This company has at least five book collections of readers theater scripts from kindergarten through grade 8.
- ➢ *Prufrock Press* (http://www.prufrock.com). This company offers two books on reader's theater with scripts appropriate for students in grades 3–4 and 4–5. Written for teachers to use with their students, these are perfect if you choose to perform as a group.
- ➢ *Teacher Created Materials* (http://www.teachercreated.com). Look for *Texts for Fluency Practice* by Rasinski and Griffith Resources. These texts are cowritten by fluency expert Timothy Rasinski for grades 1–8. As students regularly read and perform these age-appropriate texts, they improve their decoding, interpretation, and, ultimately, comprehension of the materials.

Additional commercial programs for developing reading fluency are Read Naturally (http://www.readnaturally.com) and the Marie Carbo Method (http://www.nrsi.com). Read Naturally provides a method for improving reading fluency by combining three strategies: teacher modeling, repeated reading, and progress monitoring. The Marie Carbo Method uses CDs that phrase the text in larger segments that give slower readers a chance to process the text. Readers listen to the discs three times and then they should be able to read the text back to the teacher independently. Ellen has used both of these programs with success.

App for Fluency

- ◆ *K12 Timed Reading Practice.* K12 Timed Reading Practice lets readers in levels K–4 practice fluency by reading short, timed stories. The app allows readers to focus on comprehension instead of decoding words. The app has more than 250 short stories for young readers, with a variety of fiction and nonfiction options at many different reading levels. Users can keep track of one reader's results or compile results for multiple readers. Results include the stories read, words per minute, and percent above or below average reading rates. In addition, users can get recommendations for moving up or down in reading difficulty based on their scores, or see what's next on the app's reading list.

Vocabulary

Research has emphasized that vocabulary development is a vital part of all content learning, but it is too often ignored. The link between vocabulary knowledge and comprehension is undeniable. Although reading a wide variety of material increases a student's vocabulary significantly, direct and explicit instruction in vocabulary must also occur. Parents must build word-rich environments in which to immerse their sons and teach and model good word learning strategies. Because research shows that looking up words and writing definitions is the least effective way to increase their vocabulary, parents need to use innovative and engaging activities to succeed in enhancing their son's vocabulary.

High-Frequency Vocabulary

The Dolch Sight Words are the 220 most frequently used words in the English language. These sight words make up 50%–70% of any general text. The Dolch list was developed by Dr. Edward Dolch in 1948 and published in his book *Problems in Reading*. Dolch compiled his sight word list based on the words most frequently used in children's reading books in the 1930s and 1940s. Dolch found that children who can identify a certain core group of words by sight could learn to read and comprehend better. Dolch's word lists are still widely used today and highly respected by both teachers and parents. These sight words were designed to be learned and mastered by the third grade. The list of Dolch words contains 220 words that have been arranged by levels of advancing difficulty from preprimer to third grade.

These 220 sight words include pronouns, adjectives, adverbs, prepositions, conjunctions, and verbs. In addition, there is a separate list of 95 Dolch nouns. Many of the Dolch Sight Words are difficult to portray with pictures or hard to sound out through phonics methods. Therefore, these words must be learned as sight words, and they must be quickly recognized in order to achieve reading fluency. Once children have learned and memorized these basic sight words, they read more fluently and with greater comprehension.

Word lists by level and a variety of resources for teaching high-frequency words are available for free download at http://www. uniqueteachingresources.com/reading-sight-words.html. These lists can be made into flash cards or PowerPoint slides for fluency practice. They can also be converted into a checklist to record your son's progress as he masters each list.

You can select from the following activities to reinforce students' skills with the Dolch Sight Words.

➢ *Game boards.* Create a simple game board and place the target words on each space. Roll the dice or spin a spinner. As a child lands on the space, he says the word. Provide help as needed.

➢ *Trace a high-frequency word.* Create high-frequency word game cards that use a dotted font. Let your child trace each letter. Cut out each card. Consider decorating the front of each card so you cannot see the word when playing games, or mount onto an index card or colored paper. You can also make cards using glue and sand or glitter for tactile tracing.

➢ *Word booklets.* The Hubbard's Cupboard site (http://www. hubbardscupboard.org/printable_booklets.html) provides downloadable stories that provide practice with high-frequency words. They are available for printing in black and white as well as color.

Some additional sources of high-frequency word practice include the following websites:

➢ http://www.mrsperkins.com/dolch.htm
➢ http://www.quiz-tree.com/Sight-Words_main.html
➢ http://www.candohelperpage.com/sightvocab_1.html

> ➢ http://www.samsonsclassroom.com
> ➢ http://www.msrossbec.com/sightwords.shtml

Apps for High-Frequency Words

- *Mastering Sight Words Levels 1, 2, and 3.* This app has a two-step process. Step 1, Teach Sight Words in Context, asks children to use words in sentences. When your son sees words used in sentences rather than in isolation, he is more likely to remember them. He develops an understanding of the word's meaning. Sentence-based instruction is an extremely effective method for helping children learn sight words. Step 2, Teach Sight Words Through Repetition, provides repetition of words, key to sight word acquisition. Children do not learn new sight words by being exposed to them only once. This app is specially designed to maximize word exposure.

- *Sight Word Bingo.* This app uses a barnyard theme to teach sight words. There are five difficulty levels serving preschool through grade 3. This app takes on a game format, but does not have sound during gameplay.

- *Sight Word Snapper.* This application helps kids increase their reading speed. Your son will learn to recognize sight words and will no longer be dependent on just reading words letter by letter. The app contains exercises with the 500 most frequent words in English newspapers, as well as exercises with training words consisting of 1–6, 7–10, and 11–15 letters.

- *Sight Words 2.* This app contains professional voiceovers of words for excellent auditory learning. There are five built-in games for playful learning. Hard and easy levels of difficulty for games are provided. Great memory building is achieved with the memory game in this app.

- *Sight Words Flash Cards.* The flash cards in this app are divided into four categories: preschool, kindergarten, first grade, and second grade. Each grade has an accompanying Question Mode to test and enhance reading skills. By simply clicking on the flag button provided in each flash card, you can add difficult words to the practice list for revisiting at a later time.

Comprehension

There are some requirements that have to be met before comprehension of text can occur (Block & Pressley, 2003; Pressley & Afflerbach, 1995):

➤ Good readers are active readers. They have clear goals in mind for their reading. They constantly evaluate whether the text, and their reading of it, is meeting their goals.

➤ Good readers typically look over the text before they read, noting things such as the structure of the text and text sections that might be most relevant to their reading goals. This can take the form of a picture walk through the text or a preview of chapters by older readers.

➤ As they read, good readers frequently make predictions about what is to come.

➤ They read selectively, continually making decisions about their reading—what to read carefully, what to read quickly, what not to read, what to reread, and so on.

➤ Good readers construct, revise, and question the meanings they make as they read.

➤ Good readers try to determine the meaning of unfamiliar words and concepts in the text, and they deal with inconsistencies or gaps as needed.

➤ They draw upon, compare, and integrate their prior knowledge with material in the text.

➤ They think about the authors of the text and their style, beliefs, intentions, historical milieu, and so on.

➤ They monitor their understanding of the text, making adjustments in their reading as necessary.

➤ They evaluate the text's quality and value and react to the text in a range of ways, both intellectually and emotionally.

➤ Good readers read different kinds of text differently. When reading narrative, good readers attend closely to the setting and characters. When reading expository text, these readers frequently construct and revise summaries of what they have read.

➢ For good readers, text processing occurs not only during actual reading but also during short breaks and after reading has ended.

➢ Comprehension is a consuming, continuous, and complex activity, but one that, for good readers, is both satisfying and productive.

With these requirements in mind, let us suggest a model for encouraging comprehension as you read with your son.

➢ Explain to your son that predicting is making guesses about what will come next in the text you are reading. You should make predictions often when you read. Start with the title and ask your son what he thinks the story will be about. Stop frequently as you read, discuss if your predictions were correct, and make new predictions.

➢ If he is having difficulty with predictions, model the process for him by making your own predictions. Simply say, "I am going to make predictions while I read this book. I will start with the title." Explain what you think will happen.

➢ Engage your son in collaborative predictions. Suggest that from a certain section on you want him to make predictions with you. Each of you should stop and think about what might happen next and then discuss your thoughts.

➢ After much guided practice, it is time to let your son read silently and make predictions while he reads. Remind him to be sure to make predictions often and to check as he reads to see whether his prediction came true.

Choosing Well-Suited Texts

Careful attention to the level and demands of texts used is critical. When students are first learning a comprehension strategy, they should encounter texts that do not make heavy demands in terms of extensive background knowledge, complex vocabulary, or unknown decoding skills.

The level of motivation your son brings to the text impacts whether and how he will use comprehension strategies (Dole, Brown, & Trathen, 1996; Guthrie et al., 1996). Therefore, allow the self-selection of reading material from preselected books to let his interests emerge and enhance motivation. Appendix A: Books Boys Love lists many texts that are popular with boys; for more extensive lists by subject and level, see http://www.scholastic.com/teachers/article/100-new-book-lists-created-teachers-teachers.

Activities for Comprehension

Three-Minute Pause. The Three-Minute Pause provides a chance for students to stop, reflect on the concepts and ideas that have just been read, make connections to prior knowledge or experience, and seek clarification. For a great Three-Minute Pause, take the following steps:

1. *Summarize key ideas thus far.* Can you retell the events thus far?
2. *Add your own thoughts.* What connections can be made? Does this remind you of anything that has happened to you?
3. *Pose clarifying questions.* Are there things that are still not clear? Are there confusing parts?

Graphic organizers. The purpose of a graphic organizer is to provide a visual structure for the way your son thinks about text. You probably remember the Venn diagram used to compare and contrast concepts. Your son compares things all the time. Engage in oral practice comparing and contrasting clothes, movies, and TV shows. A large assortment of graphic organizers for reading comprehension is available at http://www.scholastic.com/teachers/lesson-plan/graphic-organizers-reading-comprehension. They can be downloaded and printed. Make a complete set, then place them in page protectors or have them laminated. Then you can reuse them with each story you read. They can also be used with expository texts.

Questioning strategies. In 1956, Benjamin Bloom headed a group of educational psychologists who developed a classification of levels of intellectual behavior important in learning, called Bloom's taxonomy. The taxonomy has undergone revision since the original. It provides levels of cognition starting with basic knowledge questions in which your son will define or recall specific details in the text (remember level) and goes up to the create level. Each level of Bloom's taxonomy moves up the cognitive ladder and requires greater depth of knowledge and a higher level of critical thinking. Formulate questions at each level if possible. Even young boys can use higher order thinking skills. More information on Bloom's taxonomy is available at http://cft.vanderbilt.edu/guides-sub-pages/blooms-taxonomy.

Phrase-cued text lessons. Phrase-cued texts are a means to train students to recognize the natural pauses that occur between phrases in their reading. Because phrases are units that often encapsulate key ideas, the student's ability to identify them can enhance comprehension of the text (Rasinski, 1990, 1994). You will need two copies of a student passage: one annotated with phrase-cue marks and the other left without annotation. Guidelines for preparing phrase-cued passages include the following:

> ➤ Select a passage. Select a short (100–250 word) passage that is within the student's instructional or independent reading level.

> ➤ Mark sentence boundaries. Mark the sentence boundaries of the passage with double slashes.

> ➤ Mark within-sentence phrase breaks. Read through the passage to locate phrase breaks—naturally occurring pause points that are found within sentences. Mark each of these phrase breaks with a single slash mark. Here is an example:

The Attack of the Giant Jellyfish
/ / Big,/ huge/ jellyfish/ that can get/ up to six feet wide/ and 450 pounds/ have drifted/ into waters/ near Japan./ This/ has set off/ some big problems/ for the fishermen/ there./ The big jellyfish/ clog/ the fishing nets./ They split/ the net/ or crush/ the other fish./ Some/ of the other fish/ die/ from the stings/ of the jellyfish./ If any fish/ make it,/ they

have a lot of slime/ on them/ from the jellyfish./
This makes it hard/ to sell/ the good fish./ / /

> ➤ Provide your son with the unmarked text and show him the prepared passage with phrase-cue marks inserted.

> ➤ Read aloud your copy of the phrase-cued text. Your son follows on his copy and marks his text exactly as you have. After marking each sentence, have him read the sentence back to you and then read the entire passage from the beginning to the last sentence he has marked. This incorporates repeated reading of text as well as phrasing techniques.

> ➤ Have your son read the entire passage aloud 2–3 times. Provide ongoing feedback on his reading, noting the observance of phrase breaks. Complete the session with a retelling of the story.

Apps for Comprehension Practice

• *Aesop's Quest.* This app, based on Aesop's fables, is a learning game in which the student must remember elements of a story to complete a level. At the end of each story segment or level, the student is rewarded with puzzle pieces. After solving the puzzle, the story is complete and the child can continue to the next story. This app was developed in association with the Virginia Department of Education.

• *Fact or Opinion.* This is a Bingo-style game that helps students practice determining if a passage is factually accurate or the writer's opinion. A correct answer allows the student to place a marker on a Bingo card. Five markers in a row wins. Levels can be played in single player mode against the computer or multiplayer against a friend.

• *MiniMod Reading for Details.* Carefully aligned with the Common Core State Standards, this app helps students practice identifying the five Ws of reading—who, what, where, when, and why. Students can play in either practice mode or game mode. The game mode is a Bingo-like game. Students will read a passage about an inventor and his or her invention, then practice their understanding of reading for details. Each program offers three levels of reading difficulty that can be played in single player mode against the computer or multiplayer against a friend.

- *The Opposites.* This app helps children learn vocabulary and the corresponding antonyms by challenging them to match up pairs of opposing words at increasingly difficult levels. The game also helps children understand the importance of word context and provides an opportunity for them to think about how the words they use oppose other words. The Opposites consists of 10 different levels, each with a corresponding level of vocabulary. The app also offers a dictionary option that provides definitions and antonyms in a kid-friendly format.

- *Opposite Ocean.* Characters Luna and Leo must master the magic of words by correctly identifying the antonym of each given keyword. Children earn pearls when they drag the correct bubble word to the enchanted clam. This app was developed in association with the Virginia Department of Education.

- *Popplet.* This is a productivity app that also works as a mindmapping tool. Use the app to begin structuring the writing process, to create graphic organizers and classroom visuals, to organize material according to text structures (list, sequence, compare/contrast, cause/effect), and to practice sentence combining and complex sentence creation by connecting individual "popples."

- *Professor Garfield Fact or Opinion.* This app is part story, part game, and part online safety lesson. When Garfield's friend receives an "F" on his report about goats for using opinions instead of facts, Professor Garfield steps in to explain the differences between a fact and an opinion (particularly with regard to the Internet), how to read with a questioning mind, and how a fact can be verified. This app was developed in association with the Virginia Department of Education.

- *Question Builder.* This app is designed to help children learn to answer abstract questions and respond based on inference. Audio clips promote improved auditory processing for children with autism spectrum disorders or sensory processing disorders. Audio clip reinforcement can be turned on or off for children without special needs.

- *Same Meaning Magic.* Readers help characters Luna and Leo, young magicians at magic school, toss word stones into the wishing well to earn gold coins and jewels by choosing the best synonym. This app was developed in association with the Virginia Department of Education.

- *Same Sound Spellbound.* This app offers an adventure designed to help the player understand homophones (words that are pronounced the same but have different meanings, such as bee and be). Characters Luna and Leo, young magicians at magic school, must use their spellbook to bring animal statues to life. In the game, students must correctly identify the homophone that best completes the puzzle sentence within a given time. If the word is correct, the animal statue comes to life. If it's incorrect, the statue crumbles. This app was developed in association with the Virginia Department of Education.

- *SimpleMind.* A basic mind-mapping tool that turns your device into a brainstorming, idea-collecting, and thought-structuring device, SimpleMind's limited options make it a good tool for students who are new to mind mapping.

- *Speech With Milo.* This is a fun sequencing and storytelling game that asks students to slide the three picture cards into correct order (first, next, and last), then watch the story come to life. A speech-language pathologist chose Milo's activities, such as hitting a baseball or eating a sandwich, to help kids learn to organize time, sentence, and storytelling concepts with familiar themes. Several different Speech With Milo games are available.

Assistive Technology

With knowledge of the reading process and activity suggestions, you now have the ability to work with your son and help him practice specific reading components. Consistency of effort is critical for you and your son to achieve the desired learning outcome. To become fully literate in today's world, however, students must become proficient in the new literacies of 21st-century technologies. This is especially true for students with dyslexia who have limited access to traditional literacies.

Because information and communication technologies (ICTs) redefine the nature of literacy, it is incumbent on parents to explore these strategies and to integrate these new technologies into home-based literacy instruction.

As advocates for our children with dyslexia, it is imperative that we embrace the myriad possibilities technology has to offer. Our new instructional focus must take into consideration not only the child, his talents, his development, and his interests, but also technology possibilities. In addition, while exploring technology, we must explore the potential for circumventing our children's reading problems. By empowering our sons through access to audiovisual reference libraries, they can become proficient in gathering the information that formerly was limited to textual format. As students with dyslexia master the use of optical character recognition systems, they immediately gain independent access to multiple texts from which higher order thinking skills can be taught. Speech synthesizing technologies enable students to write into text the language they construct. These two technologies are but a sampling of the possibilities for circumventing reading and writing problems. Repeated access to these technologies will help develop writing and reading skills (Poplin, 1995).

Raskind and Higgins (1999) suggested several types of assistive technologies that allow persons with dyslexia to compensate for their disabilities rather than attempt to remediate them. These include word processing programs, spellcheckers, proofreading programs, outlining programs, abbreviation expanders, speech recognition, speech synthesis, optical character recognition systems, personal data managers, listening aids, talking calculators, digital reference books, and other interactive media and television.

Assistive technology is any device, piece of equipment, or system that helps bypass, work around, or compensate for an individual's specific learning challenges. Many more options exist today to help students and adults with learning differences make the most of their abilities. Assistive technology is not a cure for dyslexia, but it does provide alternative strategies for students to compensate for areas of weakness and capitalize on their strongest talents. For example, a student who struggles with reading but who has good listening skills might benefit from listening to audiobooks.

Assistive technology should be used in conjunction with remedial efforts and not as a replacement for remediation. As you explore assistive technology for your son, you should focus on his specific needs.

Some assistive technology tools we suggest include:

➢ *Audible.com* (http://www.audible.com). This is an Amazon. com-driven audiobook source. A huge catalog of titles provides multiple genres, including a wide range of children's literature. In addition to audiobooks, Audible.com is home to magazines, radio shows, podcasts, stand-up comedy, and speeches from modern culture, politics, and the business world. Monthly membership plans start at $14.95 after a 30-day free trial.

➢ *Bookshare* (http://www.bookshare.org). Bookshare is the world's largest online library of accessible reading materials, including books, textbooks, newspapers, and magazines, for people who have difficulties reading printed text. It allows members to find accessible titles and download them onto their personal computers. No limits are placed on the number of titles accessed at one time. Bookshare also gives users the option to read books in a browser with a screen reader or to listen to them on an mp3 player. Bookshare is free for all students with qualifying disabilities, thanks to an award from the U.S. Department of Education Office of Special Education Programs.

- ➤ *Echo Smartpen from Livescribe* (http://www.livescribe.com/en-us). Students can record everything they hear, say, and write, while linking their audio recordings to their notes. Once note-taking is completed, the student can quickly replay audio from the Livescribe paper, a computer, or a mobile device by tapping on their handwritten notes. The smartpen saves notes and recordings to a computer. This enables your son to search for words within notes.

- ➤ *Kurzweil 3000* (http://www.kurzweiledu.com/products.html). Kurzweil 3000 is a very useful comprehensive reading, writing, and learning software solution for any struggling reader, including individuals with dyslexia. The technology includes a talking word processor that reads text by word, phrase, or sentence. The speed can be controlled to meet the needs of your son.

- ➤ *Learning Ally* (formerly known as Recording for the Blind and Dyslexic, http://www.learningally.org). Learning Ally offers free individual membership for eligible people with visual impairments or dyslexia who experience difficulty in reading print material. Learning Ally's collection of more than 75,000 digitally recorded textbooks and literature titles are downloadable and accessible on mainstream as well as specialized assistive technology devices.

- ➤ *LibriVox* (http://www.librivox.org). LibriVox provides free audiobooks from the public domain. LibriVox volunteers record chapters of books in the public domain and release the audio files back onto the net. Their goal is to make all public domain books available as free audiobooks.

- ➤ *NaturalReader12* (http://www.naturalreaders.com/index.php). NaturalReader12 is an easy-to-use software that can read to your son any text from virtually any location. This includes texts contained in Microsoft Word files, webpages, PDF files, and e-mails. A free downloadable version is available on the website.

- ➤ *The Readingpen2 and Readingpen TS by Wizcom Technologies* (http://www.wizcomtech.com/eng/home/a/01/lang/index.

asp). This is a great portable learning tool for students with reading difficulties. Using the pen, the reader develops a feeling of autonomy and fluency that enhances text comprehension. Users can scan and insert text using the touch screen and virtual keyboard, hear it spoken aloud, obtain definitions, and correct pronunciations within seconds. All looked-up words can be transferred to the PC for further practice. Text can also be uploaded from the PC onto the pen, where it can be read aloud.

Assistive Technology Apps

- *Audiobooks.* This app contains more than 5,000 classic audiobooks, plus a growing collection of newer titles. A paid version is also available to eliminate ads.

- *Dragon Dictation.* This voice recognition app allows you to easily speak and instantly see your text or e-mail messages. You may need an external microphone for some devices.

- *Dragon Go!* This is an accurate way to search online content using your voice. Search queries from a variety of top websites, including Google, Yahoo, YouTube, Twitter, and Wikipedia.

- *Free Audiobooks.* This app includes best-selling and professionally narrated audiobooks; new premium titles are added monthly.

- *Image to Speech.* This app allows you to take a picture and the app will read aloud the text inside the image.

- *Jagamaga Audiobooks.* This app includes more than 200 titles, plus hundreds of free short fiction pieces; the fiction is searchable by genre, title, author, and narrator. If your son needs to read classic literature for a class, find it on your Jagamaga app and listen to it anytime on your phone. You can listen and follow along with your book and make notes.

- *Pocket.* This is a simple text-to-speech program worth exploring, as no Internet connection is needed to use it.

- *QuickVoice Recorder.* This app provides one-touch recording for memos, e-mail, dictation, lists, meetings, classes, or entire lectures.

- *Typ-O.* Typ-O uses a powerful word prediction engine and sophisticated spelling error model to help users write, even if their spelling isn't perfect.
- *Web Reader.* Web Reader uses text-to-speech technology along with web page content recognition to read web pages to users. The user can configure web pages to be read as soon as they are loaded, read pages manually after they are loaded, or use cut and paste to read only sections of text.

The Future

In the era of new literacies and new technologies, West (1991) proposed that those who are now called dyslexic may be in a position of privilege in the upcoming world. The new market for abilities and skills may increasingly devalue the conventional literate accomplishments that have carried such prestige for hundreds of years. This new market may gradually begin to reward the creative, visual-thinking dyslexics who have had such a difficult time in a traditionally literate society. It is possible that these individuals may be recognized for the talents and strengths they have always exhibited rather than being penalized or excluded.

The postliterate society will require new schools to adjust their focus to emphasize the ability to quickly access and correctly assess the implications of pertinent information, regardless of its source. Working memory limitations will be circumvented because access to information will take precedence over committing information to memory. As such trends continue, perhaps the weaknesses of people with dyslexia will come to be seen as increasingly inconsequential.

CHAPTER 7

Becoming Your Son's Advocate

You are on a journey, a crusade, a quest. Your goal is simple—to ensure that your son receives every possible legal, administrative, and educational assistance he needs in order to achieve success in the reading process. The achievement of this goal is difficult and requires a significant commitment and hard work on your part.

On your quest, you are going to have to use every persuasive tool available in your interactions with the school system. You are going to have to be better organized, clearer, more concise, and focused on your outcomes. Your controlling mantra must reflect Winston Churchill's famous words, "Never, never, never give up" until you are successful.

You need to be aware that there are no easy answers or quick solutions. Is the process difficult? Yes. Does it take a great deal of commitment and hard work? Yes. But, is it worth the effort in order to help your son be successful? Yes! So don't give up. Keep your focus on the goal: to make your son's life richer by helping him learn to read.

The first part of this chapter provides specific tips, perspectives, and strategies that will help give you a leg up as you interact with the school system. The second part provides an overview of several federal statutes and the Common Core State Standards (CCSS) initiative. A special statutory emphasis is given to the Individuals with Disabilities Education Improvement Act (IDEA). Knowledge in these areas is necessary to ensure your son receives all of the necessary support to which he is entitled under federal law.

Success Formula

As you prepare to interact with the local school system, you must focus on the outcome of ensuring that your son receives all of the appropriate educational assistance he needs. To accomplish this, it is necessary for you to understand some basic facts. First, the relationship between you and the school system is potentially adversarial by its very nature. It is essential for you to have this perspective and understanding. The school system's agenda may be quite different than yours. The opposite may also be true—you may be lucky enough to be in a school district that works hard to meet the needs of its students with special needs. Just know that this isn't always the case.

For the most part, the school system is a giant administrative morass. The goal of too many school districts is to preserve the status quo. Schools operate according to established rules and policies, many of which bear no relevance to your son's needs. They are built upon broad, generic applications of educational services that are geared to address generic kids and produce generic outcomes. They have a "one program fits all" mentality. Even the many good, sympathetic local school personnel tend to be stifled and controlled in this environment. The school system provides no incentive for them to come up with creative, individualized approaches to your son's needs. The school's policies and procedures must be followed, and your son's needs are often secondary.

Conversely, you are focused on your son as an individual. You are seeking personalized services that will address his individual needs. You are not concerned about money or effort. You just want whatever modifications necessary to help your son.

The two positions are antithetical. However, recognizing, accepting, and merging these divergent perspectives is critical to the success of your quest. It is necessary for you to be smarter, nicer, better prepared, more stubborn, more tenacious, and more committed.

Secondly, it is necessary for you to be pleasant and professional in all of your dealings with the school system. Remember the old saying, "You catch more flies with honey than with vinegar." By this point, you have probably had a long history with the school system—a long history of frustration and stunted success. Much water has passed under the bridge. Yet, you must remember that these are the very people you need to help your son with the special services and accommodations he will receive once your efforts are successful. You do not want to "win the battle, but lose the war." Your quest is not about trying to "win," to make yourself feel good, or to belittle the other side. It is not about you. It is about ensuring that your son receives the assistance necessary for his success.

You need to put your emotions aside. Use them, but harness them in a positive way to help energize you as you move through this difficult process. It does not help to raise your voice or call people names. Many of the people you will be face to face with are teachers or administrators who may well agree with you, but who are not able to officially offer support because of school policies. They likely care about your son, but they also have to comply with the system. They do not have complete flexibility, but you want to be sure they remain disposed to assist your son.

As you step into the shoes of an advocate, the road becomes a little foggy. There are times when you may be uncertain as to exactly what you want for your son. The three elements that should be your guiding principles are knowledge, clarity, and persistence. You must know the law and procedural guidelines thoroughly; you must be clear about your son's needs; and you must persist until your son has each and every service he needs to become a competent reader.

Knowledge

Never forget that knowledge is power. That is particularly true when you are attempting to get necessary educational services for your son. As we mentioned, you have to be smarter, harder working, more committed, and better prepared. But most of all, you have to be more knowledgeable about your son's needs and what rights and resources are available, as well as how your son qualifies for receipt of those resources.

Know your son. Certainly you know and love your son. But you must compile a complete factual record of your son's personal and educational profile that can be used as compelling factual support for the services you are seeking. You need to compile every document you have received from or sent to the school system or school personnel about your son. This includes all of the letters, teachers' notes, memos, e-mails, evaluations, reports, correspondence, or written documentation of any kind. Also you need all reports, evaluations, and recommendations acquired from any private professionals you might have retained.

As part of this process, you have a right to request that the school system provide you with a copy of your child's file or files, including, but not limited to, all tests, reports, assessments, protocols, grades, notes by teachers or other staff members, memos, photographs, correspondence, and so forth. In short, you need a copy of everything in your son's school files. Also, you should request copies of related and relevant documents prepared by or sent to any private professionals retained or consulted by the school system.

Next, you must be sure you understand that there is no such thing as informal communications with the school system or its personnel. All communications should be formal and in writing. For example, if you run into a teacher in the hall and have a verbal conversation relevant to your son, you should always follow up with something in writing that at a minimum repeats and confirms the relevant portions of the verbal discussions. You should also request a written confirmation from the other party.

Once you have compiled all of these documents, you need to develop a complete understanding and working knowledge of their content. You need to know, understand, and be able to refer to what each and every person has said about your son. You will likely need to retain a psychologist, educational advocate, or other professional in order to assist you with the development of a complete interpretation and understanding of technical terms, phrases, and educational jargon used in evaluations or reports related to your son.

At this point, you are ready to compile all of the documents into a file. This file must be all-inclusive. It must be organized and indexed in a manner that makes any document immediately locatable. The file needs to be easily transportable, and you should take it to every formal meeting you have with school personnel. You will be amazed by how many times you will be in a meeting and the school personnel will either not have knowledge or have incorrect knowledge of the content of some crucial document or report. Your response should be to immediately locate the relevant documents and correct any inaccuracies.

Know the law. You need to know the applicable law. In this process, it is important to recognize that a law has two parts. The first is the substantive content of the law that describes how it is applicable and what type of relief or support it provides. Secondly, laws also have a procedural component that defines the steps, requirements, and time limitation with which you must comply in order to be eligible to receive the substantive benefits under the law. You must first ensure that you comply with the procedural aspects of the law and ensure you are qualified to receive its benefits before you can evaluate those benefits.

It is essential that you read and reread the law. You must develop a working knowledge of the law that is applicable to the services you are seeking for your son. You must know what the law says and how your son qualifies under the law for the specific services you are seeking. The applicable "law" includes federal statutes, federal regulations, commentary statements in the Federal Register, and state laws, as well as administrative rules, policies, and procedures of the school system or even the local school. You must understand and address all of these.

In the last portion of this chapter, you are provided with a brief summary overview of three federal statutes that could assist you in your quest to help your son. These include the Individuals with Disabilities Education Improvement Act (2004), which provides that all children with qualifying disabilities receive a free appropriate public education designed to meet their special education needs. Also included in this chapter is a brief overview of the No Child Left Behind Act (2001). This statute provides that all children, including children with learning disabilities, have an opportunity to obtain quality, research-based reading assistance. It includes a diagnostic/assessment framework to ensure that students reach appropriate grade-level competency in a timely manner. Lastly, there is an overview of Section 504 of the Rehabilitation Act of 1973. This is a civil rights law and not a special education law. Its purpose is to use reasonable modifications or adaptations to protect disabled persons from discrimination. This includes reasonable program or procedural modifications necessary to ensure that children with learning disabilities receive an appropriate education. Although limited in both depth and breadth, the summaries of these statutes will provide you with an introduction into some of the relevant aspects of the law.

Gaining an understanding of the law and school rules or policies is not easy—it requires time and effort—but it can and must be done. In the end, you must understand the law so that you know what benefits are or are not available to your son, as well as what it takes for him to be eligible to receive them. It is up to you to ensure that your son's rights are respected.

However, it is just as important for you to know and understand the law in order to be able to rebut any inaccurate positions taken by the school system. The school system can misinterpret or misapply the law. School personnel may not fully understand it. They may not know or accurately apply the facts of your son's case to the law. When such inaccuracies happen, it is incumbent on you to step up and point out the appropriate corrections. Your file documentation on your son will allow you to correct any factual misunderstanding. However, your superior knowledge of the law and its application will give you a clear advantage in the process of persuasion.

It is necessary for you to know, use, apply, and explain your position using the applicable law's specific terminology. Accurate use of terminology is crucial to accurate outcomes. An example of this can arise if you refer your son for a private evaluation. You will need to ensure that the evaluator has a complete working understanding of the language of the law. For example, if the evaluator's report identifies the "best" educational services for your child, then the report will not be applicable to the school system's final consideration. This is because, according to the law, your child is only entitled to an "appropriate education," not the "best education." The language must be accurate.

You can obtain assistance in your efforts to understand the law from numerous sources, starting with the school system itself. IDEA requires that each school system at least once a year provide applicable parents with a notice of their rights and protections under the law. However, you also have the right to simply request a copy. You should also check because most school systems make a copy of this document available online.

There are also many local parent support groups and organizations. There are educational advocates, legal advocates, countless articles, and websites that provide a plethora of information and explanation, including:

> *Electronic Code of Federal Regulations* (http://www.ecfr.gov). This site provides the full text of various statutes and regulations, as well as text and Boolean search capabilities within the text.

> *Families and Advocates Partnership for Education* (http://www.fape.org). This organization provides information and training on IDEA and related topics at workshops, brown bag seminars, satellite video conferences, and online training. The site includes referrals to national, state, and local disability organizations and advocates and to a nationwide network of parent training and information centers and community parent resource centers. Information on research about best practices that can be used to improve educational services is also available.

> *National Center for Learning Disabilities* (http://www.ncld.org). This site connects parents to important resources, articles, links, and guides for learning disabilities, dyslexia, and special education services. It also offers a "Parents Guide to Dyslexia,"

identifies educational rights and opportunities, and shares topical videos, articles, and links.

➤ *Parent to Parent USA* (http://www.p2pusa.org). Administered through local and state organizations, this group provides emotional and informational support to families of children who have special needs, most notably by matching parents seeking support with an experienced, trained "Support Parent." The site provides training, reference resources, and referrals.

➤ *Wrightslaw* (http://www.wrightslaw.com). This is an excellent resource on all topics related to special education. It includes topical information, legal libraries incorporating a vast array of resources on legal issues, cases, and regulations, and commentaries regarding applicable laws. Multiple website links on all relevant topics, plus a newsletter, DVDs, books, and live seminars are offered.

Know school system personnel. You need to know the school system personnel who will be making the decisions regarding the special services you are seeking for your son. You are entitled to notice of any scheduled meetings, including an identification of who will attend. Review the attendance list carefully. It is important for you to know who you are meeting with and what his or her orientation is with regard to such issues. Look through the attendance list and immediately identify the persons you know. You need to prepare a brief written dossier on each. Know who might be receptive to your position and helpful to your quest. Although his or her ability to publicly support you may be limited, such support behind closed doors could be crucial. Find out how the individuals on your child's team have decided in previous cases and the specific concerns that they have raised that you will need to address. But remember, if the services you seek will greatly increase the workload of an individual or cause her to be in disfavor with her bosses for bucking the status quo, she may be less than excited about your requests. As for any persons you do not know, find out about them. Learn their positions and their prior responses to the type of issues you are raising. Talk to parents who have been through the process of seeking similar services for their child. They may be able to provide real insight as to the orientation of your child's team members. Lastly, write down the information you gain and review it before each meeting.

Clarity

In the movie *Cool Hand Luke*, the old prison warden keeps telling Paul Newman's inmate character (who continually challenges the prison's rules), "What we've got here is a failure to communicate." Unfortunately, many fights, arguments, divorces, and even wars arise from a failure of two sides to effectively communicate. In this process with the school system, it is absolutely essential that you have done all of the difficult work of learning the law and learning your son's complete history. However, once all of the hard work is done, it is of no value unless you can communicate clearly and precisely to the school system what you want for your son and why he is entitled to it.

Be prepared to provide input during your son's Individualized Education Program (IEP) meeting. Your time to present at your child's case meeting will be short and the other members' attention span will be even shorter. You need to distill your entire claim—facts and law— into a 5-minute "elevator speech." Your orientation and identification must be concise and accurate. Further, you are only going to get what you ask for, so be sure to specifically identify the assistance you are seeking. Your statements should include:

➤ your son's specific needs;
➤ the factual basis and identification of the documents that support the needs you identify;
➤ the specific portions of each law that identify what accommodations or services to which your son is entitled;
➤ the specific reasons why the school system's profile of your son and representation of the law are inaccurate; and
➤ specifically what assistance, services, or accommodations you are seeking for your son.

Attending meetings. It is vitally important that you attend each and every meeting. The school system personnel must give you timely notice of every meeting, and they have an obligation to make every effort to ensure that the meetings are held at a time and place that are convenient for you.

It is critical for you to actively inject yourself into the discussions and decisions. If you are not present, the process will move on without you, and decisions will be made with which you might not agree. You will have no chance to control the outcomes. However, if you attend the meetings, and if you have followed all of the ideas we have addressed and done all of your homework, then you will be the person at the meeting who can provide the most accurate and complete history of your son, as well as the most accurate interpretation of the law. You will have the knowledge. You will have the power. You will be able to control and direct favorable outcomes from the meeting. Use the opportunities meetings present to set, on the record and with school system personnel, specific, objective outcomes reached or to be reached along with specific dates for their accomplishment.

Personal journal. You should keep a private comprehensive journal that chronicles each and every aspect of your quest. This should include meetings, findings, recommendations, outcomes, and personnel involved. It is for your use only. However, it will allow you to have a quick, comprehensive review of all that has previously transpired. From meeting to meeting, participating school personnel may change and not know the complete prior history; they might misstate the prior occurrences, or they may have forgotten. By reviewing your journal before each meeting, you will be able to maintain and convey a consistent, accurate account of what has been accomplished to date. You will not have to back up and redo what has already been done. Again, knowledge is power and by having such information you will make yourself the indispensable participant in the process.

Taping meetings. Buy a small, pocket-size digital recorder. You are not trying to be secretive. Before each meeting begins, you should openly state that you intend to record it. Put the recorder right out on the table.

This action is important for a couple of reasons. First, it is intimidating and will require the school system personnel to be careful and measured in what they say and do. Secondly, it will allow you the opportunity to have a complete, accurate record of what was said and decided upon. You will then need to have these recordings transcribed so that you have an accessible record of the proceedings. These transcripts will afford you the opportunity to review the meeting, address uncertainties, and plan for the future. Many school systems record meetings themselves. On their assurance that you can receive a copy of the recording, you might be willing to forgo your taping efforts. However, such a waiver of your rights is not recommended. You need to maintain control over the information. This is the only way you can ensure that the information is retained, accurately transcribed, and available in a timely manner to you.

Notes. Even though you are taping the proceedings, you want to take notes during the meeting of issues that have special importance. Specifically, you want to write down any stated findings or recommendations. Before the meeting ends, read your notes to the group, and be sure your reading is included in the minutes. Then, make sure you have a confirmation of their accuracy on the record before the meeting adjourns.

Minutes. Before the close of the meeting, you should request a copy of the minutes and a copy of the outcomes of the meeting. When received, the formal minutes need to be verified against your taped transcription. This is the best way to ensure the completeness and accuracy of the school system's records.

Persistence

We cannot stress the need to be an advocate more than this: This is about your son. This is about your son's future. This is about your son's life. This is about ensuring your son receives the support and services necessary to guarantee his success. It is the most important thing you can do.

As previously indicated, you must maintain a professional attitude. You must be nice in every way, but at the same time, you must make noise. You must be aware of what is going on with your child every day. You must ask questions and raise issues. Whenever school system personnel look at your son, they should know that their every action or nonaction will be reviewed. They should feel a positive level of discomfort. They should feel the accountability of having someone looking over their shoulder. You need to be a polite person who will be there every day, asking the hard questions, fighting the status quo, and working tirelessly for your son.

You may encounter significant pushback as you work to assert your son's rights. But you must not be deterred, embarrassed, or intimidated, and don't accept no for an answer. If you've done your homework, then you will know more about your son's needs and rights under the law than anyone in the school system. Hang in there with the professionals—be bold. Don't stop, don't lose your focus, and never give up.

The Law

The remaining portions of this chapter provide a very limited overview of several federal laws that are potentially applicable to your quest. Neither the laws nor the summaries are in any way intended to be all-inclusive.

The primary emphasis addresses the Individuals with Disabilities Education Improvement Act (IDEA; 2004). This is the primary statute for special education and related services for children with identified learning disabilities. However, also included in this chapter are very limited overviews of the No Child Left Behind Act (NCLB; 2001) and Section 504 of the Rehabilitation Act of 1973. Although these statutes have a broad reach, they can work in conjunction with IDEA to offer educational standards, processes, and procedures, as well as supportive services, for qualifying disabled children. However, do not forget that there exists a plethora of federal and state laws, as well as local policies, procedures, and guidelines that also address issues that support children's educational services.

This material can seem technical and dry. It is not necessarily an "easy read." But your quest is not an easy one, either. To ensure success, you must read, understand, evaluate, and develop a complete working knowledge of the primary sources of this information.

Overview of Individuals With Disabilities Education Improvement Act of 2004

Special education law for children with disabilities finds its roots in 1975 with the passage of the Education for all Handicapped Children Act. Since that time, the law has been amended and changed several times, with the most recent iteration being the Individuals with Disabilities Education Improvement Act (2004), or IDEA. Congress identified the purpose of IDEA as ensuring that all children with disabilities have available to them a free appropriate public education (FAPE) that emphasizes their unique needs and prepares them for further education, employment, and independent living. In addition, IDEA ensures that the rights of children with disabilities and parents of such children are protected. The primary funding mechanism for IDEA comes from federal grants to the states. While assisting the states in the provision of special education and related services, IDEA also allows the respective states control over the application of many aspects of the education process.

Special education services provided under IDEA require specifically designed instructional goals and procedures intended to meet the unique needs of eligible children with disabilities. Further, these services are to be provided at no cost to the parents. IDEA also includes a comprehensive system of procedural safeguards designed to engage parents and ensure their participation in the educational decisions made for their child with disabilities. Further, IDEA provides parents with the availability of a comprehensive administrative and judicial due process review of any decisions with which they disagree. IDEA has four main parts:

- ➢ Parts A and B cover eligibility procedures, regulations, and required educational services for children with disabilities between the ages of 3–21.
- ➢ Part C pertains to services for infants and toddlers with disabilities under the age of 3.
- ➢ Part D discusses national activities that have been promoted to enhance educational services for children with disabilities.

Your focus as a parent seeking services under IDEA will be on Parts A and B. Under these portions of IDEA, a free appropriate public education is made available to all qualifying disabled children between the ages of 3 and 21. To be eligible, a child must be identified as having a disability defined under IDEA, including a specific learning disability such as dyslexia. Eligible children receive special education and related services under an Individualized Education Program (IEP). The IEP identifies a child's educational status, the specific nature of any disability, and individualized services, as well as annual, academic, and functional goals and measures used to track a child's progress.

Special Education Services

IDEA lists 13 specific categories of disabilities that are covered and that qualify a child to receive special education services. Aside from these specifically identified categories of qualifying disabilities, a child is eligible for special education and related services under IDEA if he has a specific learning disability. A specific learning disability is defined as a disorder of one or more of the basic psychological processes involved in understanding or using spoken or written language. According to IDEA, this includes dyslexia.

Evaluations to determine your son's needs. Before initiating special education and related services under IDEA for a child suspected of having a disability that interferes with his ability to learn, the local educational agency (LEA) must conduct a full, comprehensive, and individualized evaluation of the child. The request for an initial evaluation can be made by either the parents or the LEA. An LEA proposing to conduct such an evaluation must provide proper notice to the parents. The notice must fully describe why the evaluation is to be conducted, the nature and extent of any proposed evaluation procedures, as well as an identification of each action that is being proposed.

Aside from providing notice, the LEA must also obtain informed parental consent, or at least make every reasonable effort to obtain an informed consent, before it proceeds with such an evaluation. If the parents fail to respond to such a request or refuse to provide consent for the evaluation process, then the requesting LEA may attempt to obtain parental consent through procedural safeguards under IDEA. The initial evaluation should consist of evaluative tools necessary to determine whether or not the child has a qualifying disability, as well as the child's educational needs in light of such a disability. Upon the completion of the assessments and other evaluative measures, the parents and a group of qualified professionals on the evaluation team determine whether the child has a qualifying disability under IDEA, as well as the educational needs of the child. In the compilation and interpretation of the evaluation information, the LEA is required to draw upon a variety of sources, including aptitude and achievement tests, parental input, and teacher recommendations. If it is determined that the child has a disability and is entitled to special education and related services under IDEA, then an IEP must be developed for the child. A copy of the evaluation report and the documentation of the potential eligibility determination must be provided to the child's parents.

The compilation and evaluation of this broad spectrum of information will help to ensure that the child's IEP reflects accurate information regarding the child's current educational status, his or her needs, the specific nature of any disability, and individualized services to be provided to the child. Such a complete assessment picture of the child will assist in the identification and development of annual academic and functional goals and measures used to identify the child's progress toward goal attainment.

What Happens When Your Son Qualifies for Special Education and Related Services Under IDEA

The determination that a child qualifies for special education services under IDEA must be made by the child's parents and a "team of qualified professionals." The team must include the child's "regular teacher" or a classroom teacher qualified to teach children the same age as the child. Also included should be at least one person qualified to conduct individual diagnostic evaluations such as a school psychologist, speech-language pathologist, or remedial reading teacher.

This determination is based upon the existence of a qualifying specific learning disability. The decision is supported by all evaluative data collected, including research-based interventions. Data can include, but are not limited to, documentation that shares:

- ➤ that the child has a specific learning disability;
- ➤ the basis for making the determination;
- ➤ the relevant behavior noted during the observation of the child and the relationship of the behavior to academic functioning;
- ➤ any educationally relevant medical findings;
- ➤ that the child does not exhibit age-appropriate achievement or meet, or make sufficient progress toward, state-approved grade-level standards or intellectual development;
- ➤ if the child participated in the Response to Intervention (RtI) process that assessed the child's response to scientific, research-based intervention;
- ➤ the instructional strategies used, the student-centered data collected, and the child's response to the scientific research-based intervention provided as part of the child's participation in the RtI process;
- ➤ that the child's parents were notified about the state's policies regarding the amount and nature of student performance data that would be provided;
- ➤ educational services that would be provided;
- ➤ strategies for increasing the child's rate of learning; and
- ➤ the parents' right to request an evaluation.

Individualized education programs. Once a child's qualifying disability is properly identified, IDEA requires that an IEP be developed. An IEP team is responsible for the creation and implementation of the child's IEP. This team includes the parents, special education and regular teachers, and a representative of the LEA, as well as an individual who can interpret the instructional implications of any evaluation results.

In developing a child's IEP, the team must consider the strengths of the child, the concerns of the parents, the results of the initial or most recent evaluation, as well as the academic, developmental, and functional needs of the child (IDEA, 2004). Also, if necessary, the team must consider the appropriateness of any positive behavioral interventions, supports, and strategies to address any behavioral issue that potentially interferes with the child's success under the IEP.

The IEP document is a child's individualized "game plan" or "road map" for services under IDEA. IDEA is very specific as to what information must be included in an IEP. The requirements include, but are not limited to, an identification of the child's present level of academic achievement and functional performance, a statement of measurable annual academic and functional goals, a description of benchmarks or short-term objectives, and a statement of any appropriate individual accommodations.

The LEA is also charged with conducting periodic reviews of a child's IEP in order to evaluate the achievement of progress toward the identified goals, as well as any needed amendments. Such a review should be conducted no less than annually. The IEP should be revised as necessary to address any lack of progress toward these goals and any additions or modifications that need to be made in order to enable to child to attain the identified goals (IDEA, 2004).

Make no mistake about it, if your son is determined to be eligible for special education services under IDEA, an accurate and appropriate IEP is required for his ultimate success. Therefore, it is critical for you to go to the law to learn and understand what IDEA requires to be included in an IEP. Then, as a parent and member of the IEP team, you must insert yourself into the process. You must ensure the sufficiency of the IEP's content, its accuracy as it relates to your son's history, and its concordance with the law. Do not approve or sign off on the document until all of your concerns have been addressed.

Procedural Safeguards

Parental participation. Parents of a disabled child are required members of any group empowered to make decisions regarding the special education services or related placement of their child. IDEA mandates that prior notice be provided to the parents of the purpose, time, and location of any meetings. The notice must also include the identification and professional credentials of the persons who will attend. If neither parent can personally attend a scheduled meeting, the LEA must attempt to use other methods in order to facilitate their participation. This can include conference calls, Skyping, or video conferencing. If, despite all documented efforts, the local agency is unable to obtain the parents' participation, then the group may move forward with its decisions.

Independent educational evaluations. If the parents of a child with a qualifying disability under IDEA (2004) disagree with the evaluation obtained by the LEA, they have the right to request an independent educational evaluation of their child at public expense. If the LEA does not approve the free independent evaluation requested by the parents, the parents always have the right to obtain an evaluation at their own expense. If the parents obtain such an independent educational evaluation at public expense or share with the LEA an evaluation obtained at private expense, the results of the evaluation must be considered in any decisions related to the provision of special education and related services to the child.

Parental notice. The LEA must provide the parents of a child with a disability with reasonable, timely, written notice if the LEA either proposes to initiate changes or refuses to initiate changes in the identification, evaluation, or educational placement of the child. IDEA is very specific as to the nature and content of the information or explanations contained in such a notice.

Procedural safeguards notice. A notice of procedural safeguards under IDEA is a written notice of a child's rights and procedural remedies available under the law. IDEA requires that a copy of this notice be given to the parents of a qualifying disabled child at least once a school year. However, additional copies must also be provided to the parents upon the initial referral of a child, upon the parents' request for an evaluation, upon the filing of a due process complaint, or at the request of the parents.

It is absolutely critical that you are aware of all of the rights and remedies available to your son under IDEA. You must obtain a copy of this document every year.

Mediation. The LEA must ensure that procedures are in place to allow disputes to be resolved through a mediation process. The mediation process must be voluntary on the part of both parties, not used to deny or delay any party's rights, and must be conducted by a qualified mediator. The state must bear the cost of any mediation process. If the parties successfully resolve their dispute through the mediation process, then they must execute a legally binding settlement agreement. Although the agreement is admissible and binding in any subsequent court action, the actual discussions during the mediation process remain totally confidential and may not be subsequently divulged.

Filing a due process complaint. The parents of a disabled child or the LEA may file a "due process complaint" that addresses any alleged violation of IDEA as it related to the identification, evaluation, or educational placement of their child or the provision of an appropriate education. In general, such alleged violations are limited to those that occurred not more than 2 years before the complaining party knew or should have known that they occurred.

IDEA identifies very specific information that must be included in such a complaint. The applicable state department of education is required to develop and make available to parents model forms to assist in the drafting and filing of a due process complaint. However, use of these forms is not required. All that is required is that the due process complaint as filed must comply with the stated requirements identified in IDEA.

There are a number of time limitations and specific procedural requirements related to both the filing of a due process complaint, the response to the complaint, and additional related resolution processes. If you intend to file such a complaint, then you need to carefully review the applicable section of IDEA and ensure that you are in full compliance with all substantive and procedural requirements.

Impartial due process hearing. If the issues identified in a due process complaint cannot be informally resolved by the parties, then a due process hearing is conducted by an impartial hearing officer. This is a formal hearing on the issues identified in the due process complaint. It is governed by the specific rules of administrative procedures (Logsdon, n.d.). The hearing process involves the production of documentary evidence, witness testimony, and the cross-examination of witnesses. Subject to the dictates of the applicable formal administrative procedures, each party has the right to be accompanied by legal counsel or persons with knowledge and training with regard to children with disabilities.

It should be noted that a legal advocate may provide invaluable assistance to you at this stage of the proceedings. As indicated, it is a formal hearing process based upon established administrative procedures. The LEA will likely be represented by its legal counsel. Thus, the litigation experience of such an advocate could be beneficial. Further, if the party's dispute has gone this far without resolution, the introduction of a legal advocate would likely do little to aggravate the already heightened adversarial relationship.

Hearing decision and appeals. The parents are entitled to a copy of any decision by the hearing officer. Any such decision is subject to possible appeal by either party. The appeal process includes, if allowed under applicable state law, an appeal to the applicable state board of education. However, once all applicable administrative appeals have been exhausted, either party may appeal the hearing officer's decision to the applicable federal court.

Disciplinary Issues

Parents of children with learning disabilities know all too well that their child's learning frustrations can manifest themselves as behavioral issues. IDEA provides protections and limitations with regard to the nature and extent of disciplinary actions the LEA may apply to a child with disabilities. In general, school personnel may remove a child with a disability who violates a code of student conduct to an appropriate interim alternative educational setting or another setting, or suspend the child for not more than 10 consecutive school days (to the same extent applicable to children without disabilities). Any additional removals of not more than 10 consecutive days in the school year for separate incidents of misconduct are allowed subject to limitations. IDEA requires that after a child with a disability has been removed from his current placement for 10 days, any subsequent removals during the same year require the LEA to provide services that enable the child to continue participating in the general curriculum and continue progress toward the IEP goals. Also, the child must receive a functional behavioral assessment (FBA), behavioral intervention services, and modifications designed to address the behavior involved so that it does not reoccur.

Within 10 days of any decision to change the placement of a child with a disability because of a violation of a code of student conduct, the local agency, the parents, and the relevant members of the IEP team must determine if the conduct in question was caused by, or had a direct and substantial relationship to, the child's disability, or if it was a direct result of the LEA's failure to implement the child's IEP. If a determination is made that the behavior in question was a manifestation of the child's disability, then the IEP team must conduct an FBA and see that it is implemented. If a behavioral assessment has already been conducted, then it is to be reviewed and modified as appropriate.

IDEA also contains an identification of special circumstances behaviors that include things such as possession of weapons or illegal drugs and serious bodily injury to another at school, on school property, or at a school function. Such an occurrence would allow for the removal of the disabled child to an alternate setting for not more than 45 days. This can be accomplished without regard to whether or not the behavior is determined to be a manifestation of the child's disability.

On the date that the decision is made to make a change of placement of a child with a disability because of a violation of the student code of conduct, the LEA must notify the parents. The parents are also entitled to a procedural safeguards notice as identified in IDEA. These safeguards also allow the parents a right to appeal any disciplinary placement. A disabled child who qualifies for special education services under IDEA remains entitled to these services even if he is expelled from school for disciplinary reasons.

Child Placed in a Private School or Facility

There are three basic scenarios that can result in a child receiving special education services under IDEA even though he is enrolled in private or religious schools, based on the time and agency of the child's placement. The first relates to children who have been enrolled by their parents in a private school, the second to children removed from public education by their parents in favor of private education, and the third to children placed in private schools by the LEA itself.

In the first instance, IDEA's "child find process" requires the LEA to locate, identify, and evaluate all children with disabilities who have been enrolled by their parents in private or religious schools operating in the LEA's district. The child find process requires his equitable participation in similar special education and related services as provided by the LEA to public school children. The LEA makes the final decision with respect to the nature and extent of any IDEA services to be provided to these private school children. In this regard, it must be remembered that no such privately placed child has an individual right to receive special education or related services and, in fact, any services provided may differ in amount and content from those received by children in public schools. However, a "services plan" that is compliant with the IEP requirements of IDEA is to be developed and implemented for these children. To ensure the development of a timely and meaningful plan, the LEA is required to consult with the child's parents and the appropriate private school representatives. LEA funds may not be used to support existing needs of the private school or its students. However, subject to availability, the LEA may make funds available to hire public school personnel, or even private school personnel, in order to provide the needed support services of these students.

The second scenario relates to a child who is receiving special education and related services under IDEA in a public school but the parents decide that in order for their child to receive an appropriate education, they must move their child to a private school. In such cases, the child is not eligible to receive special education and related services or reimbursement of any private school costs unless the parents can show, through consent of the LEA or a favorable ruling from a due process hearing, that the move is necessary for their child to receive an "appropriate education." Such a ruling can be difficult to obtain. Likewise, it is often hard to convince LEAs of the necessity of private placement, as it would mean admitting the inadequacies of their offerings in respect to your son. IDEA (2004) also contains a number of specific statutory procedural limitations that can derail the success of any such efforts.

In order to maximize your chances of success, you should make every effort to work closely with the LEA in order to ensure full transparency and maximize the possibility of full cooperation. However, it is recommended that if you are seeking financial assistance for a private educational relocation of your son, you should strongly consider obtaining information, consultation, and guidance from a professional special education advocate. Such professional guidance can be crucial to maximizing your success possibilities, and success will more than repay any costs you might incur.

Lastly, the situation arises from time to time where the LEA may determine that a student's need for special education programs and services can only be met by placing the child in a private or religious school. Such a placement can be accomplished in compliance with the child's IEP and at no cost to the parents. Students placed in private schools by the LEA have the same rights and entitlement to services as their counterparts attending public schools (IDEA, 2004).

No Child Left Behind Act of 2001 and Section 504 of the Rehabilitation Act of 1973

The primary focus in this chapter has been on IDEA. However, there are other legislative sources of educational support for children with learning disabilities. It is important to recognize and understand how each complements or interfaces with IDEA in order to provide educational assistance to children with learning disabilities, including reading problems. The various laws include, but are not limited to, the No Child Left Behind Act (NCLB; 2001) and Section 504 of the Rehabilitation Act of 1973. Although not written specifically for children with disabilities, NCLB provides for scientifically based reading instruction and evaluation directed toward the assurance that all children reach appropriate grade-level performance in a timely manner, as well as support services for children who need additional assistance to reach these goals.

Section 504 prohibits discrimination against persons with disabilities when those disabilities interfere with life functions, including learning. Identified disabilities can include learning disabilities. Section 504 provides for the provision of significant accommodations in the learning process to assist disabled children. The following outline of relevant portions of these two acts helps to identify how these laws relate to, interfere with, or support IDEA and children with learning disabilities.

No Child Left Behind Act of 2001

NCLB (2001) is a reauthorization of the Elementary and Secondary Education Act (1965). It provides federal money to public schools to be used toward achievement of accountability-based educational achievement goals (Education Week, 2011). NCLB has to be reauthorized every 5 years. However, the original authorization expired in 2007 and Congress has been funding NCLB through extensions ever since. Sweeping changes have been proposed to NCLB and, at this time, a number of states have been granted waivers that allow for a delay/modification of a number of NCLB requirements (Rothstein, 2009).

NCLB supports standards-based educational reform centered on the premise that setting high standards and measurable goals can improve individual outcomes in education. NCLB requires states to develop assessments in basic skills and to assess all students at selected grade levels in order to receive the applicable federal school funds. NCLB does not assert a national achievement standard. However, NCLB expanded the federal role in public education through annual testing of academic progress, report cards, teacher qualifications, and funding changes (Education Week, 2011).

With regard to its support for the reading process, NCLB differs from IDEA and Section 504 in that a child is not required to have a formal diagnosis of a disability in order to receive benefits under the law. Children who struggle with reading tend to fall behind their nondisabled peers most and profit the most from NCLB's assistance (Marshall, 2004).

The purpose of NCLB (2001) is to ensure that all children have a fair, equal, and significant opportunity to obtain a quality education and reach, at a minimum, proficiency as determined by academic standards and academic assessment tools. To accomplish this stated purpose, NCLB puts a high priority on promoting reading achievement and requires that schools establish reading programs that are founded upon scientifically based reading research. This is research that relies on scientific measurements and observational methods of collecting data. The stated goal is to ensure that every student can read at grade level or above not later than the end of grade 3 (Margolin & Buchler, 2004). NCLB defines reading as a complex system of deriving meaning from print that includes:

> ➤ the skills and knowledge to understand how phonemes, or speech sounds, are connected to print;
> ➤ the ability to decode unfamiliar words;
> ➤ the ability to read fluently;
> ➤ sufficient background information and vocabulary to foster reading comprehension;
> ➤ the development of appropriate active strategies to construct meaning from print; and
> ➤ the development and maintenance of a motivation to read.

NCLB requires that reading programs must provide explicit and systematic instruction in the areas of phonemic awareness, phonics, vocabulary development, reading fluency (including oral reading skills), and reading comprehension strategies. The improvement process under these reading programs is achieved through the application of scientifically based reading research. This process:

> ➤ applies rigorous, systematic, and objective procedures to obtain valid knowledge relevant to reading development, reading instruction, and reading difficulties;
>
> ➤ includes research that employs systematic, empirical methods that draw on observation or experiment;
>
> ➤ involves rigorous data analysis that are adequate to test the stated hypotheses and justify the general conclusions drawn;
>
> ➤ relies on measurements or observational methods that provide valid data across evaluators and observers and across multiple measurements and observations; and
>
> ➤ have been accepted by a peer-reviewed journal or approved by a panel of independent experts through a comparably rigorous, objective, and scientific review. (NCLB, 2001, 20 U.S.C. 6368(6))

NCLB creates time-relevant achievement goals for your child's development of reading proficiency. Specifically, it requires that all children read on grade level no later than the end of the third grade. NCLB identifies the essential components of reading instruction. It also requires that reading programs use scientifically based reading research in order to provide explicit and systematic instruction in the areas of phonemic awareness, phonics, vocabulary development, reading fluency (including oral reading skills), and reading comprehension strategies. NCLB offers supplemental services often given by private providers, including some programs geared specifically to students with dyslexia (Marshall, 2004).

NCLB is certain to undergo significant changes and modifications in the next few years. However, at this time, the majority of the proposed modifications (and the multiple waivers that have been issued to multiple states) have been directed primarily toward the accountability/measurability/sanctions arising from the achievement/accountability portions of the law. The instructional portions of NCLB have been subjected to fewer changes. Thus, at this time (and until changed), it is important to recognize that NCLB provides potentially significant reading assistance to your child. Unless it is changed, NCLB puts a high priority on promoting reading achievement (Marshall, 2004). It should also be noted that several states and districts throughout the country have received waivers from the federal government to develop their own, different guidelines subject to federal approval. It is imperative that you research the guidelines applicable to your local district and the resources available if they differ from the federal standard.

Section 504 of the Rehabilitation Act of 1973

Section 504 of the Rehabilitation Act of 1973 is not a special education law. It is a civil rights law that is intended to prevent discrimination against persons with a disability by institutions receiving or benefiting from public funds. It defines an individual with a disability as a person who has a physical or mental impairment that limits one or more major life activity. The protected major life activities include, but are not limited to, "learning" and are applicable to "specific learning disabilities." As a general rule, if a child is eligible for services under IDEA (2004), he or she qualifies for protection under Section 504. However, not all students covered under Section 504 are eligible for IDEA services. Section 504 has a much broader definition of disabilities and so it applies to more people (National Center for Learning Disabilities, 2006).

Section 504 provides that no individual or student with a disability shall be discriminated against because of that disability. The law provides that all disabled students are entitled to a free appropriate public education. Such a free appropriate public education requires the provision of regular or special education aids and service designed to adequately meet the educational needs of students with disabilities to the same extent the needs of nondisabled students are met.

Parents seeking to have their children receive appropriate educational support with regard to a learning disability should submit a written notice to the LEA requesting an evaluation to determine if the child has a disability under Section 504 that presents a significant impact on the child's ability to learn. This request should be submitted to the LEA's Section 504 Coordinator and the principal (who usually serves as the coordinator). You should include in your request copies of any evaluations or medical documentation you have that support your request. This request document should be hand-delivered or at a minimum sent via registered mail. In addition to parental initiation of such requests, a referral can come from anyone, including a school nurse, teachers, counselor, or any professional familiar with the child's accommodation needs. In fact, the child can even make a self-referral request.

It is important to recognize that the procedures related to the handling of a Section 504 request are local in nature. Therefore, you should obtain a copy of your school district's policies and procedures related to Section 504. These documents will help inform you of your rights and the school's rights and responsibilities in the provision of the necessary accommodations (National Center for Learning Disabilities, 2006).

Evaluation reviews under Section 504 must draw from a variety of sources (National Center for Learning Disabilities, 2006). Ultimately, a group decision is made by persons with knowledge of the child, applicable evaluation data, and consideration of available reasonable educational accommodations (National Center for Learning Disabilities, 2006). It is important to note that parents are not required by law to be a part of this decision-making process, but are often included by the LEA. The LEA is required to develop a reasonable plan to accommodate the child's disability and remove any barriers that might prevent the child from participating fully in the programs and services provided through the general curriculum. This plan does not have to be in writing. Although an IEP is not required under Section 504, if the child is also eligible under IDEA, then in most cases, the IEP will be an inclusive substitute for the Section 504 plan. Although the final plan does not require parental consent, the LEA is required to provide notice to the parents of the plan decided upon (Council for Exceptional Children, 2002).

The LEA is required to develop a reasonable plan to accommodate the child's disability and remove any barriers that might prevent the child from fully participating in the general curriculum. Some examples of the kinds of reasonable modifications or adaptations that might be provided under Section 504 for children with learning disabilities include things such as (Council for Exceptional Children, 2002):

➤ *Presentation.* Provide audio tapes, large print, oral instructions, repeat directions;

➤ *Response.* Allow verbal responses, a scribe to record response, response via computer, tape recorder;

➤ *Timing/scheduling.* Allow frequent breaks, extend time allotments;

➤ *Setting.* Provide special seating, small group setting, private room; and

➤ *Equipment and material.* Provide calculator, amplification equipment, manipulatives.

Local educational agencies must also provide for impartial hearings for parents who disagree with their child's identification, evaluation, or placement. Although parents must have an opportunity to participate and be represented by counsel if they choose, under Section 504 the hearing's procedural details and parents' rights are left to the discretion of the LEA (Council for Exceptional Children, 2002).

Common Core Initiative

The Common Core Initiative (Common Core) is not a program created by the federal government. Common Core actually found its genesis with the states' governors through the National Governors Association Center for Best Practices and state school officials through the Council of Chief State School Officers. There are two separate components applicable to Common Core. First, there are the "standards." The creators of Common Core consider these to be the culmination of extensive, broad-based efforts to create the next generation of K–12 common curriculum standards. Participating states are required to adjust their primary and secondary school curricula for English/language arts and literacy in history/social studies, science, and technical subjects in order to comply (Schoof, 2013; National Governors Association Center for Best Practices [NGA] & Council of Chief State School Officers [CCSSO], 2011).

Common Core contends that the standards are intended as goals and not mandates. Their purpose is to support student learning through the provision of more clarity, consistency, and an equal exposure to the learning experiences in the various states' curricula. These are to result in a coordination of what is expected of all K–12 students across the country and the provision of an equal opportunity for an education regardless of where they live. As a result of the application of these standards, all students are to be college and career ready no later than the end of high school (NGA & CCSSO, 2011; Schoof, 2013).

The second component of Common Core consists of a testing assessment component. This purpose of this process serves to identify performance exception standards for students in kindergarten through 12th grade. To accomplish this outcome, Common Core provides yearly testing of grades 3–8 and once in high school. This testing function is grounded in common performance principles that will allow for comparison across students, schools, districts, states, and the entire country. Such broad applicability of outcomes is intended to assist in the creation of educational economies of scale, support more effective teaching and learning, and better prepare students for their future college or career efforts (NGA & CCSSO, 2011).

At this time, more than 40 states and the District of Columbia have adopted the Common Core State Standards (CCSS) to some extent. However, it is significant to note that the federal government has contributed significant financial efforts to incentivize the states to accept the standards. In fact, some people have gone so far as to say that these incentives were used to "railroad" the states into acceptance. The incentives include favorable consideration of a state's application for the very lucrative Race to the Top education grants and greater likelihood postponing the application of the harsher NCLB achievement standards through favorable consideration of their NCLB waiver requests (Elbow, 2013; Ravitch, 2013; Strauss, 2013a; Toppo, 2012).

Despite the broad initial acceptance of CCSS by most states, the actual implementation and funding of the initiatives at the state level have run into significant political, public, and educational opposition.

Opponents cite a number of issues that they contend represent fatal flaws in the initiative.

First, many opponents believe that education is a state function and that the states themselves know how to best educate their children. They contend that the broad national nature of the CCSS and the broad national application of the assessment outcomes constitute a "federal curriculum" and deprive the states of their ability to shape and control the exercise of these basic state functions (Bidwell, 2013; Trianni, 2013; The Trouble with Common Core, 2013). Thus, while "proponents say Common Core will help establish national education standards, critics believe it will mean the end of local control of education" (Chiaramonte, 2013).

Secondly, it is difficult to garner public, political, or educational support for the significant resource expenditures required by CCSS implementation. CCSS requires local school districts to completely overhaul their entire curricula, purchase new compliant textbooks and instructional materials, expand teacher training, and acquire broad technological upgrades and training in order to ensure compliance. States are having trouble finding resources and justifying these extensive new expenditures, especially at a time when teachers are being laid off and basic student programs are being cut (Bidwell, 2013; Parker, 2013; Trianni, 2013).

Thirdly, strong and vocal opposition remains as to what is considered the imposition of the CCSS from "above" with only minimal engagement of the very people who are responsible for its implementation—the public, state school boards, teachers, or parents. Opponents are adamant that such a program should not micromanage the classroom and mandate to teachers what and how they should teach (Hess, 2012; Ravitch, 2013; Strauss, 2013a). Teachers have said that the CCSS has combined with pressure to "teach to the test" to take all individuality out of the classroom. A New Jersey teacher said that the rigid new standards have left teachers feeling like "robots." She said, "I was given a curriculum and told by my administration to teach it 'word-for-word'" (Chiaramonte, 2013, para. 11).

Lastly, opponents and supporters alike point out that despite extensive federal support for Common Core, and the significant monetary investments surrounding its development and implementation, no one knows if these new initiatives will actually help students learn. This is because the CCSS has never undergone "field testing" (Trianni, 2013; Strauss, 2013b).

The extent to which the Common Core initiative may be ultimately accepted or implemented by the states, as well as the final form that Common Core may take, remains to be seen. Although a number of states have approved Common Core, a number of other states are considering, or even pursuing, limitations or repeal of their participation (Parker, 2013; Strauss, 2013b). In fact, all that is clear at this point is that the answers to these questions and the ultimate outcomes appear to have moved even farther into the blurry, unpredictable political arena. What you can be sure of is that the final outcome of these issues, whatever they might be, will likely have a significant impact on your son's education. You need to make yourself aware of this debate, the issues involved, and the potential final outcomes. Then, regardless of your position, you must actively participate in this dialogue in order to ensure a positive outcome for your son.

References

American Psychiatric Association. (2013). *Diagnostic and statistical manual of mental disorders* (5th ed.). Washington, DC: Author.

Baddeley, A. D., & Hitch, G. I. (1974). Working memory. In G. H. Bower (Ed.), *The psychology of learning and motivation: Advances in research and theory* (Vol. 8, pp. 47–89). New York, NY: Academic Press.

Badian, N. A. (2005). Does a visual-orthographic deficit contribute to reading disability? *Annals of Dyslexia, 55,* 28–52.

Bassok, D., & Reardon, S. (2013). "Academic redshirting" in kindergarten: Prevalence, patterns, and implications. *Educational Evaluation and Policy Analysis, 35,* 283–297.

Beers, K. G. (1996). Choosing not to read: Understanding why some middle schoolers just say no. In K. G. Beers & B. G. Daniels (Eds.), *Into focus: Understanding and creating middle school readers* (pp. 37–63). Norwood, MA: Christopher-Gordon.

Bidwell, A. (2013). States lack resources, funds to implement common core. *U.S. News and World Report.* Retrieved from http://www.usnews.com/news/articles/2013/08/07/states-lack-resources-funds-to-implement-common-core

Blachman, B. A., Ball, E. W., Black, R., & Tangle, D. M. (2000). *Road to the code: A phonological awareness program for young children.* Baltimore, MD: Brookes.

Black, A., & Stave, A. M. (2007). *A comprehensive guide to readers theatre: Enhancing fluency and comprehension in middle school and beyond.* Newark, DE: International Reading Association.

Block, C. C., & Pressley, M. (2003). Best practices in comprehension instruction. *Best Practices in Literacy Instruction, 2,* 111–126.

Bos, C., Mather, N., Dickson, S., Podhajski, B., & Chard, D. (2001). Perceptions and knowledge of preservice and in-service educators about early reading instruction. *Annals of Dyslexia, 51*(1), 97–120.

Bronson, P., & Merryman, A. (2013). *Top dog: The science of winning and losing.* New York, NY: Random House.

Brown, M. (2013, October). Neil Gaiman: Let children read the books they love. *The Guardian.* Retrieved from http://www.theguardian.com/books/2013/oct/14/neil-gaiman-children-books-reading-lecture

Chall, J. (1983). *Stages of reading development.* New York, NY: McGraw Hill.

Chiaramonte, P. (2013). Teachers complain Common Core-linked lessons little more than scripts to read. *Fox News.* Retrieved from http://www.foxnews.com/us/2013/12/08/teachers-complain-common-core-linked-lessons-little-more-than-scripts-to-read/

Christakis, E. (2013, February). Do teachers really discriminate against boys? *Time.* Retrieved from http://ideas.time.com/2013/02/06/do-teachers-really-discriminate-against-boys/

Cornwell, C., Mustard, D. B., & Van Parys, J. (2013). Noncognitive skills and the gender disparities in test scores and teacher assessments: Evidence from primary school. *Journal of Human Resources, 48*(1), 236–264.

Council for Exceptional Children. (2002). Understanding the differences between IDEA and Sec. 504. *Teaching Exceptional Children, 34*(3). Retrieved from http://ldonline.org/article/6086

Davies, B. (2003). *Shards of glass: Children reading and writing beyond gendered identities.* Cresshill, NJ: Hampton Press.

Dole, J. A., Brown, K. J., & Trathen, W. (1996). The effects of strategy instruction on the comprehension performance of at-risk students. *Reading Research Quarterly, 31*(1), 62–88.

Dyslexia Institutes of America. (2014). *Types of dyslexia.* Retrieved from http://dyslexiainstitutes.com/?page=types

Education for All Handicapped Children Act of 1975. Pub. Law 94-142. (November 29, 1975).

Education Week. (2011). *No child left behind.* Retrieved from http://www.edweek.org/ew/issues/no-child-left-behind

Ehri, L. C., & McCormick, S. (2004). Phases of word learning: Implications for instruction with delayed and disabled readers. In R. B. Ruddell & N. J. Unrau (Eds.), *Theoretical models and processes of reading* (5th ed., pp. 339–361). Newark, DE: International Reading Association.

Eicher, J. D., & Gruen, J. R. (2013). Imaging-genetics in dyslexia: Connecting risk genetic variants to brain neuroimaging and ultimately to reading impairments. *Molecular Genetics and Metabolism, 110,* 201–212.

Elementary and Secondary Education Act of 1965, §142, 20 U.S.C. 863.

Elbow, S. (2013, September). Common Core standards also under attack from the left. *The Cap Times.* Retrieved from http://host.madison.com/news/local/writers/steven_elbow/common-core-standards-also-under-attack-from-the-left/article_63041aff-a415-5c82-bdfc-f6ccc2d5d5a3.html

Frith, U. (1999). Paradoxes in the definition of dyslexia. *Dyslexia, 5,* 192–214.

Flynn, R. M. (2007). *Dramatizing the content with curriculum-based readers theatre, grades 6–12.* Newark, DE: International Reading Association.

Forgan, J. W., & Richey, M. (2012). *Raising boys with ADHD: Secrets for parenting healthy, happy sons.* Waco, TX: Prufrock Press.

Gaub, M., & Carlson, C. (1997). Gender differences in ADHD: a meta-analysis and critical review. *Journal of the American Academy of Child and Adolescent Psychiatry, 8,* 1036–1045.

Gidwitz, A. (2010). *Frequently asked questions.* Retrieved from http://www.adamgidwitz.com/faq-questions-inline

Goodman, K. S. (1967). Reading: A psycholinguistic guessing game. *Journal of the Reading Specialist, 6,* 126–135.

Gurian, M., & Stevens, K. (2004). With boys and girls in mind. *Educational Leadership, 62*(3), 21–26.

Guthrie, J. T., Meter, P., McCann, A. D., Wigfield, A., Bennett, L., Poundstone, C. C., & Mitchell, A. M. (1996). Growth of literacy engagement: Changes in motivations and strategies during concept-oriented reading instruction. *Reading Research Quarterly, 31,* 306–332.

Harvey, S., & Goudvis, A. (2000). *Strategies that work: Teaching comprehension to enhance understanding* (Vol. 372). York, ME: Stenhouse Publishers.

Hess, F. M. (2012, December 11). Enforcing conformity is risky. *The New York Times.* Retrieved from http://www.nytimes.com/roomfordebate/2012/12/10/the-american-way-of-learning/enforcing-common-core-standards-would-be-risky

Hook, P. E., & Jones, S. D. (2002). The importance of automaticity and fluency for efficient reading comprehension. *Perspectives, 28*(1), 9–14.

Individuals with Disabilities Education Improvement Act, 20 U.S.C. 1400 et seq. (2004)

International Dyslexia Association. (2014). *What is dyslexia?* Retrieved from http://www.interdys.org/DyslexiaDefinition.htm.

Juel, C., & Minden-Cupp, C. (2004). Learning to read words: Linguistic units and instructional strategies. In R. B. Ruddell & N. J. Unrau (Eds.), *Theoretical models and processes of reading* (5th ed., pp. 313–364). Newark, DE: International Reading Association.

Keehn, S., Harmon, J., & Shoho, A. (2008). A study of readers theater in eighth grade: Issues of fluency, comprehension, and vocabulary. *Reading & Writing Quarterly, 24,* 335–362.

Kohn, A. (1992). *No contest: The case against competition.* New York, NY: Houghton Mifflin Harcourt.

Kyllonen, P., & Christal, R. (1990). Reasoning ability is (little more than) working memory capacity?! *Intelligence, 14,* 389–433.

LaBerge, D., & Samuels, S. J. (1974). Toward a theory of automatic information processing in reading. *Cognitive Psychology, 6,* 293–323.

Lahey, J. (2013, June). Stop penalizing boys for not being still in school. *The Atlantic.* Retrieved from http://www.theatlantic.com/sexes/archive/2013/06/stop-penalizing-boys-for-not-being-able-to-sit-still-at-school/276976/

Lave, J., & Wenger, E. (1991). *Situated learning: Legitimate peripheral participation.* New York, NY: Cambridge University Press.

Lin, A. (2008). *Problematizing identity: Everyday struggles in language, culture, and education.* New York, NY: Lawrence Erlbaum.

Logsdon, A. (n.d.). Special education due process hearing. Retrieved from http://learningdisabilities.about.com/od/disabilitylaws/a/due_process_hea.htm

Logue, M. E., & Harvey, H. (2010). Preschool teachers' views of active play. *Journal of Research in Childhood Education, 24*(1), 32–49.

Madden, M., & Allen, E. J. (2006). Chilly classrooms for female undergraduate students: A question of method? *The Journal of Higher Education, 77*(4), 684–711.

Margolin, J., & Buchler, B. (2004). *Critical issue: Using scientifically based research to guide educational decisions.* Retrieved from http://www.ncrel.org/sdrs/areas/issues/envrnmnt/go/go900.htm

Marshall, A. (2004a). *No child left behind.* Retrieved from http://www.netplaces.com/parenting-kids-with-dyslexia/additional-legal-protections/no-child-left-behind.htm

McDermott, R., Goldman, S., & Varenne, H. (2006). The cultural work of learning disabilities. *Educational Researcher, 35*(6), 12–17.

Moats, L. C. (1994). The missing foundation in teacher education: Knowledge of the structure of spoken and written language. *Annals of Dyslexia, 44*(1), 81–102.

Moats, L. C. (1999). *Teaching reading is rocket science: What expert teachers of reading should know and be able to do.* Washington, DC: American Federation of Teachers.

Moloney, L. (2002). Coming out of the shed: Reflections on men and fathers. *Australian and New Zealand Journal of Family Therapy, 23*(2), 69–78.

Morrow, L., & Gambrell, L. (2011). *Best practices in literacy instruction.* Urbana, IL: National Council of Teachers of English.

Morrow, L. M., Gambrell, L. B., & Duke, N. K. (Eds.). (2011). *Best practices in literacy instruction*. New York, NY: Guilford Press.

National Center for Education Statistics. (2014). *NAEP long-term trend assessments*. Retrieved from http://nces.ed.gov/nationsreportcard

National Center for Learning Disabilities. (2006). *Accommodations for students with LD*. Retrieved from http://www.ldonline.org/article/Accommodations_for_Students_with_LD

National Council on Teacher Quality. (2013). *2014 teacher prep review*. Retrieved from http://www.nctq.org/siteHome.do

National Governors Association Center for Best Practices, & Council of Chief State School Officers. (2011). *Common Core State Standards initiative*. Retrieved from http://www.nga.org/cms/home/special/col2-content/common-core-state-standards-init.html

National Institute of Child Health and Human Development. (2000). *Report of the National Reading Panel. Teaching children to read: An evidence-based assessment of the scientific research literature on reading and its implications for reading instruction* (NIH Publication No. 00-4769). Washington, DC: U.S. Government Printing Office.

National Institutes of Health. (2007, November). *Brain matures a few years late in ADHD, but follows normal pattern*. Retrieved from http://www.nimh.nih.gov/news/science-news/2007/brain-matures-a-few-years-late-in-adhd-but-follows-normal-pattern.shtml

National Institute of Mental Health. (2013). *What is Attention Deficit Hyperactivity Disorder (ADHD, ADD)?* Retrieved from http://www.nimh.nih.gov/health/topics/attention-deficit-hyperactivity-disorder-adhd/index.shtml#part3

Neuman, S. B., & Dickinson, D. K. (Eds.). (2001). *Handbook of early literacy research* (Vol. 1). New York, NY: Guilford.

No Child Left Behind Act, 20 U.S.C. §6301 (2001).

Nöthen, M. M., Schulte-Körne, G., Grimm, T., Cichon, S., Vogt, I. R., Müller-Myhsok, B., . . . & Remschmidt, H. (1999). Genetic linkage analysis with dyslexia: Evidence for linkage of spelling disability to chromosome 15. *European Child and Adolescent Psychiatry, 8*, 56–59.

Olulade, O., Napoliello, E., & Eden, G. (2013). Abnormal visual motion processing is not a cause of dyslexia. *Neuron, 79*(1), 180–190.

Orton, S. (1919). On the classification of nervous and mental diseases. *The American Journal of Psychiatry, 76,* 131–144.

Parker, S. (2013, July). *The unraveling of the Common Core.* Retrieved from http://www.takepart.com/article/2013/07/26/are-common-core-standards-already-falling-apart

Poplin, M. (1995). The dialectic nature of technology and holism: The use of technology for the liberation of the learning disabled. *Learning Disability Quarterly, 18,* 131–140.

Pressley, M. (2002). *Reading instruction that works: The case for balanced teaching* (2nd ed.). New York, NY: Guilford.

Pressley, M., & Afflerbach, P. P. (1995). *Verbal protocols of reading: The nature of constructively responsive reading.* New York, NY: Routledge.

Rabiner, D., & Coie, J. D. (2000). Early attention problems and children's reading achievement: A longitudinal investigation. *Journal of the American Academy of Child & Adolescent Psychiatry, 39,* 859–867.

Rasinski, T. V. (1990). A brief history of reading fluency. In S. J. Samuels & A. E. Farstrup (Eds.), *What research has to say about fluency instruction* (pp. 4–23). Newark, DE: International Reading Association.

Rasinski, T. V. (1994). Developing syntactic sensitivity in reading through phrase-cued texts. *Intervention in School and Clinic, 29,* 165–168.

Raskind, M., & Higgins, E. (1999). Speaking to read: The effects of speech recognition technology on the reading and spelling performance of children with learning disabilities. *Annals of Dyslexia, 49,* 251–281.

Ravitch, D. (2013, August 24). *The biggest fallacy of the Common Core Standards: No evidence* [Web log post].Retrieved from http://dianeravitch.net/2013/08/24/the-biggest-fallacy-of-the-common-core-standards-no-evidence

Reichert, M., & Hawley, R. (2010). *Reaching boys, teaching boys: Strategies that work—and why.* San Fransisco, CA: Jossey Bass.

Renaissance Learning. (2014). *Accelerated reading.* Retrieved from http://www.renaissance.com/

Rothstein, R. (2009). *The prospects for no child left behind.* Retrieved from http://www.epi.org/publication/pm149

Samuels, S. J. (1979). The method of repeated readings. *The Reading Teacher, 32,* 403–408.

Sax, L. (2013). *Boys adrift: The five factors driving the growing epidemic of unmotivated boys and underachieving young men.* New York, NY: Basic Books.

Schoof, R. (2013, June 10). Separating fact from fiction about Common Core education standards. *McClatchyDC.* Retrieved from http://www.mcclatchydc.com/2013/06/10/193328/separating-fact-from-fiction-about.html

Section 504 of the Rehabilitation Act, 29 U.S.C. Section 76 et. Seq. (1973).

Shaywitz, S. E. (2003). *Overcoming dyslexia: A new and complete science-based program for reading problems at any level.* New York, NY: Vintage.

Shaywitz, S. E., Fletcher, J. M., Holahan, J. M., Schneider, J. E., Marchione, K. E., . . . Shaywitz, B. A. (1999). Persistence of dyslexia: The Connecticut longitudinal study at adolescence. *Paediatrics, 104,* 1351–1359.

Sloyer, S. (1982). *Readers theatre: Story dramatization in the classroom.* Urbana, IL: National Council of Teachers of English.

Smith, M. W., & Wilhelm, J. D. (2002). *"Reading don't fix no Chevys": Literacy in the lives of young men.* Portsmouth, NH: Heineman.

Snow, C. E., Burns, M. S., & Griffin, P. (Eds.). (1998). *Preventing reading difficulties in young children.* Washington, DC: National Academy Press.

Snow, C. E., & Juel, C. (2005). *Teaching children to read: What do we know about how to do it?* Indianapolis, IN: Blackwell.

Sommers, C. H. (2013, August). School has become too hostile to boys. *Time.* Retrieved from http://ideas.time.com/2013/08/19/school-has-become-too-hostile-to-boys/

Stanovich, K. E. (2000). *Progress in understanding reading: Scientific foundations and new frontiers.* New York, NY: Guilford.

Stone, J., & Harris, K. (1991). These coloured spectacles: What are they for? *Support for Learning, 6,* 116–118.

Straight, S. (2009). Reading by the numbers. *The New York Times Book Review.* Retrieved from http://www.nytimes.com/2009/08/30/books/review/Straight-t.html/?_r=0

Strauss, V. (2013a, February 26). Why I oppose Common Core standards: Ravitch. *The Washington Post.* Retrieved from http://www.

washingtonpost.com/blogs/answer-sheet/wp/2013/02/26/
why-i-oppose-common-core-standards-ravitch

Strauss, V. (2013b, April 24). Is the Common Core Standard Initiative
in trouble? *The Washington Post.* Retrieved from http://www.
washingtonpost.com/blogs/answer-sheet/wp/2013/04/24/
is-the-common-core-standards-initiative-in-trouble

Sullivan, M. (2003). *Connecting boys with books: What libraries can do.*
Chicago, IL: American Library Association.

Szatmari, P. (1992). The epidemiology of attention-deficit hyperactivity disorder. *Child and adolescent psychiatry clinics of North America, 1,*
361–371.

Texas child suspended after hugging aide. (2006). Retrieved from http://
www.nbcnews.com/id/16159302/ns/us_news-education/t/
texas-child-suspended-after-hugging-aide

Toppo, G. (2012, May 1). Common Core standards drive wedge
in education circles. *USA Today.* Retrieved from http://usa-
today30.usatoday.com/news/education/story/2012-04-28/
common-core-education/54583192/1

Trianni, F. (2013). States struggle to fund stricter school curriculum: Study. *Reuters.* Retrieved from http://www.reuters.
com/article/2013/08/07/us-usa-education-study-idUSBRE
97616720130807

The Trouble with the Common Core. (2013). *Rethinking Schools,*
27(4). Retrieved from http://www.rethinkingschools.org/
archive/27_04/edit274.shtml

Tyre, P. (2008). *The trouble with boys: A surprising report card on our sons, their*
problems at school, and what parents and educators must do. New York, NY:
Crown.

West, T. G. (1991). *In the mind's eye: Visual thinkers, gifted people with learn-*
ing disabilities, computer images, and the ironies of creativity. Buffalo, NY:
Prometheus Books.

Worthy, J., & Prater, K. (2002). The intermediate grades: "I thought
about it all night": Readers theatre for reading fluency and motivation. *The Reading Teacher, 56,* 294–297.

Zull, J. E. (2004). The art of changing the brain. *Educational Leadership,*
62(1), 68–72.

Books Boys Love

Picture Books

The Adventures of Sparrowboy by Brian Pinkney
Alexander and the Terrible, Horrible, No Good, Very Bad Day by Judith Viorst
Animalia by Graeme Base
Bugs! Bugs! Bugs! by Bob Barner
Click, Clack, Moo: Cows That Type by Doreen Cronin
Cloudy With a Chance of Meatballs by Judi Barett
Dragons Love Tacos by Adam Rubin
Everyone Poops by Taro Gomi
Freight Train by Donald Crews
The Great Truck Rescue (Jon Scieszka's Trucktown) by Jon Scieszka
Harold and the Purple Crayon by Crockett Johnson
Honk That Horn! (Jon Scieszka's Trucktown) by Justin Spelvin
Jamberry by Bruce Degen
Jumanji by Chris Van Allsburg
Little Granny Quarterback by by Bill Martin Jr. and Michael Sampson
No, David! by David Shannon

Patrick's Dinosaurs by Carol Carrick

Pete's a Pizza by William Steig

Pierre: A Cautionary Tale in Five Chapters and a Prologue by Maurice Sendak

Press Here by Herve Tullet

Shark vs. Train by Chris Barton

Snow Trucking! (Jon Scieszka's Trucktown) by Jon Scieszka

Superhero ABC by Bob McLeod

Swish! by Bill Martin Jr. and Michael Sampson

Take a Trip With Trucktown! (Jon Scieszka's Trucktown) by Justin Spelvin

Trucks Line Up (Jon Scieszka's Trucktown) by Jon Scieszka

Uh-Oh, Max! (Jon Scieszka's Trucktown) by Jon Scieszka

Grades 2–5

The Adventures of Captain Underpants series by Dav Pilkey

The Dangerous Book for Boys by Conn Iggulden and Hal Iggulden

Danny the Champion of the World by Roald Dahl

Dirty Beasts by Roald Dahl

George's Marvelous Medicine by Roald Dahl

James and the Giant Peach by Roald Dahl

A Nation's Hope: The Story of Boxing Legend Joe Louis by Matt de la Peña

Revolting Rhymes by Roald Dahl

Solomon Snow and the Silver Spoon by Kaye Umansky

Solomon Snow and the Stolen Jewel by Kaye Umansky

The Stinky Cheese Man and Other Fairly Stupid Tales by Jon Scieszka

The Twits by Roald Dahl

The Witches by Roald Dahl

The World According to Humphrey series by Betty Birney

Grades 3–7

Be a Perfect Person in Just Three Days! by Stephen Manes

Bone: The Complete Cartoon Epic in One Volume by Jeff Smith

Diary of a Wimpy Kid series by Jeff Kinney

The Egypt Game by Zilpha Keatley Snyder

Evolving Planet: Four Billion Years of Life on Earth by Erica Kelly and
    Richard Kissel

Fablehaven by Brandon Mull

The Fairy Tale Detectives (Sisters Grimm series) by Michael Buckley

George's Secret Key to the Universe by Lucy Hawking and Steven Hawking

Gregor the Overlander (Underland Chronicles series) by Suzanne Collins

Horten's Miraculous Mechanisms: Magic, Mystery, and a Very Strange Adventure
    by Lissa Evans

How to Eat Fried Worms by Thomas Rockwell

How to Train Your Dragon by Cressida Cowell

The Incredible Adventures of Professor Branestawm by Norman Hunter

The Indian in the Cupboard by Lynne Reid Banks

The Invention of Hugo Cabret by Brian Selznick

The Last Hero by Terry Pratchett

Minecraft: The Essential Handbook

The Orphan of Awkward Falls by Keith Graves

The Phantom Tollbooth by Norton Juster

Splendors and Glooms by Laura Amy Schlitz

Sports Camp by Rich Wallace

The Stonekeeper (Amulet series) by Kazu Kibuishi

Ten Rules You Absolutely Must Not Break if You Want to Survive the School Bus
    by John Grandits

The Trumpet of the Swan by E.B. White

Grades 5–9

The Absolutely True Diary of a Part-Time Indian by Sherman Alexie

The Amazing Maurice and His Educated Rodents by Terry Pratchett

Bad Island by Doug TenNapel

Barbarian Lord by Matt Smith

Cardboard by Doug TenNapel

Dragonbreath by Ursula Vernon

Ender's Game by Orson Scott Card

Gear by Doug TenNapel

Ghostopolis by Doug TenNapel
The Graveyard Book by Neil Gaiman
The Great Greene Heist by Varian Johnson
Hatchet by Gary Paulsen
I Am the Messenger by Markus Zusak
The Illustrated Man by Ray Bradbury
I, Robot by Isaac Asimov
Iron West by Doug TenNapel
Jing: King of Bandits by Yuichi Kumakura
The Lightning Thief (Percy Jackson and the Olympians series) by
     Rick Riordan
The Maze Runner series by James Dashner
Nation by Terry Pratchett
Peter Nimble and His Fantastic Eyes by Jonathan Auxier
The Ruins of Gorlan (Ranger's Apprentice series) by John Flanagan
The Storm in the Barn by Matt Phelan
Tailchaser's Song by Tad Williams
A Tale Dark and Grimm series by Adam Gidwitz
Tommysaurus Rex by Doug TenNapel
A Wizard of Earthsea (Earthsea Cycle series) by Ursula LeGuin

Grades 9–12

100 Sideways Miles by Andrew Smith
An Abundance of Katherines by John Green
Angry Young Man by Chris Lynch
Ball Don't Lie by Matt de la Peña
Boot Camp by Todd Strasser
The Brave by Robert Lipsyte
The Chocolate War by Robert Cormier
The Contender by Robert Lipsyte
Death by Black Hole and Other Cosmic Quandaries by Neil deGrasse Tyson
Ghost Medicine by Andrew Smith
The Gospel of Winter by Brendan Kiely
Grasshopper Jungle by Andrew Smith

How to Teach Relativity to Your Dog by Chad Orzel
Inexcusable by Chris Lynch
It's Kind of a Funny Story by Ned Vizzini
I Will Save You by Matt de la Peña
The Living by Matt de la Peña
Looking for Alaska by John Green
Mexican WhiteBoy by Matt de la Peña
The Nazi Hunters by Neal Bascomb
No Place by Todd Strasser
One Fat Summer by Robert Lipsyte
Paper Towns by John Green
Passenger by Andrew Smith
Raiders Night by Robert Lipsyte
Ready Player One by Ernest Cline
Stick by Andrew Smith
Tanker 10 by Jonathan Curelop
V for Vendetta by Alan Moore
Watchmen by Alan Moore
We Were Here by Matt de la Peña
Will Grayson, Will Grayson by John Green and David Levithan
Winger by Andrew Smith

Glossary of Reading Terms

Accuracy (part of fluency): reading words in text with no errors.

Academically engaged: when students are participating in activities or instruction in a meaningful way and understanding the tasks in which they are involved.

Advanced phonics: strategies for decoding multisyllabic words that include morphology and information about the meaning, pronunciation, and parts of speech of words gained from knowledge of prefixes, roots, and suffixes.

Affix: a general term that refers to prefixes and suffixes.

After Reading Comprehension strategies: strategies that require the reader to actively transform key information in text that has been read (e.g., summarizing, retelling).

Aligned materials: student materials (e.g., texts, activities, manipulatives, homework) that reinforce classroom instruction of specific skills in reading.

Alliteration: the repetition of the initial phoneme of each word in connected text (e.g., Harry the happy hippo hula-hoops with Henrietta).

Alphabetic principle: the concept that letters and letter combinations represent individual phonemes in written words.

Ample opportunities for student practice: when students are asked to apply what they have been taught in order to accomplish specific reading tasks. Practice should follow in a logical relationship with what has just been taught. Once skills are internalized, students are provided with more opportunities to independently implement previously learned information.

Analogy: comparing two sets of words to show some common similarity between the sets. When done as a vocabulary exercise, this requires producing one of the words (e.g., cat is to kitten as dog is to ___).

Antonym: a word opposite in meaning to another word.

Automaticity: reading without conscious effort or attention to decoding.

Background knowledge: forming connections between the text and the information and experiences of the reader.

Base word: a unit of meaning that can stand alone as a whole word (e.g., friend, pig); also called a free morpheme.

Before Reading Comprehension strategies: strategies employed to emphasize the importance of preparing students to read text (e.g., activate prior knowledge, set a purpose for reading).

Blending: the task of combining sounds rapidly to accurately represent the word.

Bloom's taxonomy: a system for categorizing levels of abstraction of questions that commonly occur in educational settings; includes the following competencies: knowledge, comprehension, application, analysis, synthesis, and evaluation.

Chunked text: continuous text that has been separated into meaningful phrases, often with the use of single and double slash marks (/ and

//). The intent of using chunked text or chunking text is to give children an opportunity to practice reading phrases fluently. There is no absolute in chunking text. Teachers should use judgment when teaching students how to chunk. Generally, slash marks are made between subject and predicate and before and after prepositional phrases.

Chunking: a decoding strategy for breaking words into manageable parts (e.g., /yes /ter/ day). Chunking also refers to the process of dividing a sentence into smaller phrases where pauses might occur naturally (e.g., when the sun appeared after the storm, / the newly fallen snow / shimmered like diamonds).

Coaching: a professional development process of supporting teachers in implementing new classroom practices by providing new content and information, modeling related teaching strategies, and offering ongoing feedback as teachers master new practices.

Coarticulation: when saying words our mouth is always ready for the next sound to be made. While saying one sound, the lips, tongue, etc., are starting to form the sound to follow. This can distort individual sounds during speech because the sounds are not produced in isolated units (e.g., ham—the /m/ blends with the /a/ to distort the vowel). Because of coarticulation, some children have difficulty hearing the individual sounds in words, and the concept of phonemes needs to be explicitly brought to their attention through instruction.

Cognates: words that are related to each other by virtue of being derived from a common origin (e.g., "decisive" and "decision").

Coherent instructional design: a logical, sequential, plan for delivering instruction.

Comprehension: understanding what one is reading, the ultimate goal of all reading activity.

Comprehensive/Core Reading Program (CRP): the initial instructional tool teachers use to teach children to learn to read, including instruction in the five components of reading identified by the National Reading Panel (phonemic awareness, phonics, fluency, vocabulary, comprehension), spelling, and writing to ensure they reach reading levels that meet or exceed grade-level standards. A CRP should address the instructional needs of the majority of students in a respective school or district.

Comprehensive Intervention Reading Program (CIRP): these programs are intended for students who are reading one or more years below grade level, and who are struggling with a broad range of reading skills. Comprehensive Intervention Programs include instructional content based on the five essential components of reading instruction integrated into a coherent instructional design. A coherent design includes explicit instructional strategies, coordinated instructional sequences, ample practice opportunities and aligned student materials. Comprehensive Intervention Programs provide instruction that is more intensive, explicit, systematic, and more motivating than instruction students have previously received. These programs also provide more frequent assessments of student progress and more systematic review in order to ensure proper pacing of instruction and mastery of all instructional components.

Comprehension monitoring: an awareness of one's understanding of text being read. Comprehension monitoring is part of metacognition, or "thinking about thinking." A reader should know what is clear and what is confusing and have the capabilities to make repairs to problems with comprehension.

Comprehension questions: questions that address the meaning of text, ranging from literal to inferential to analytical.

Concept definition mapping: provides a visual framework for organizing conceptual information in the process of defining a word or concept. The framework contains the category, properties, and examples of the word or concept.

Connected text: words that are linked (as opposed to words in a list), as in sentences, phrases, and paragraphs.

Consonant blend: two or more consecutive consonants which retain their individual sounds (e.g., /bl/ in block; /str/ in string).

Consonant digraph: two consecutive consonants that represent one phoneme, or sound (e.g., /ch/, /sh/).

Context clue: using words or sentences around an unfamiliar word to help clarify its meaning.

Continuous sounds: a sound that can be held for several seconds without distortion (e.g., /m/, /s/).

Continuum of word types: words can be classified by type according to their relative difficulty to decode. Typically this continuum is listed from easy to difficult, beginning with VC and CVC words that begin with continuous sounds and progressing to CCCVC and CCCVCC words.

Coordinated instructional sequences: take into consideration how information is selected, sequenced, organized, and practiced. Coordinated instructional sequences occur within each component of reading where a logical progression of skills would be evident: easier skills are introduced before more difficult skills, so that skills build progressively. The other way coordinated instructional sequences are evident is in the clear and meaningful relationship or linking of instruction across the five components of reading: phonological awareness, phonics, fluency, vocabulary, comprehension. If students orally segment and blend words with the letter-sound /f/ during phonemic awareness instruction, then we would expect to see it followed by practice in connecting the sound /f/ with the letter f. This would be followed by fluency practice in reading words, sentences, and/or passages with the letter-sound /f/. Spelling practice would include /f/ and other previously learned letter-sounds.

Core instruction: instruction provided to all students in the class, and it is usually guided by a comprehensive core reading program. Part of the core instruction is usually provided to the class as a whole, and part is provided during the small-group differentiated instruction period. Although instruction is differentiated by student need during the small-group period, materials and lesson procedures from the core program can frequently be used to provide reteaching, or additional teaching to students according to their needs.

Cumulative: instruction that builds upon previously learned concepts.

Decodable text: text in which a high proportion of words (80%-90%) comprise sound-symbol relationships that have already been taught. Used for the purpose of providing practice with specific decoding skills and is a bridge between learning phonics and the application of phonics in independent reading.

Decodable words: words that contain phonic elements that were previously taught.

Decoding: the ability to translate a word from print to speech, usually by employing knowledge of sound-symbol correspondences; also the act of deciphering a new word by sounding it out.

Derivational affix: a prefix or suffix added to a root or base to form another word (e.g., -un in unhappy , -ness in likeness).

Diagnostic: tests that can be used to measure a variety of reading, language, or cognitive skills. Although they can be given as soon as a screening test indicates a child is behind in reading growth, they will usually be given only if a child fails to make adequate progress after being given extra help in learning to read. They are designed to provide a more precise and detailed picture of the full range of a child's knowledge and skill so that instruction can be more precisely planned.

Dialogic reading: when, during story reading, the teacher or parent asks questions, adds information, and prompts student to increase sophistication of responses by expanding on his utterances.

Differentiated instruction: matching instruction to meet the different needs of learners in a given classroom.

Difficult words: some words are difficult because they contain phonic elements that have not yet been taught; others are difficult because they contain letter-sound correspondences that are unique to that word (e.g., yacht).

Digraphs: a group of two consecutive letters whose phonetic value is a single sound (e.g., /ea/ in bread; /ch/ in chat; /ng/ in sing).

Diphthong: a vowel produced by the tongue shifting position during articulation; a vowel that feels as if it has two parts, especially the vowels spelled ow, oy, ou, and oi.

Direct instruction: the teacher defines and teaches a concept, guides students through its application, and arranges for extended guided practice until mastery is achieved.

Direct vocabulary instruction: planned instruction to preteach new, important, and difficult words to ensure the quantity and quality of exposures to words that students will encounter in their reading.

During Reading Comprehension strategies: strategies that help students engage the meanings of a text (e.g., asking questions at critical junctures, modeling the thought process used to make inferences, constructing mental imagery).

Elkonin boxes: a framework used during phonemic awareness instruction, sometimes referred to as sound boxes. When working with words, the teacher can draw one box per sound for a target word. Students push a marker into one box as they segment each sound in the word.

Emergent literacy: the skills, knowledge, and attitudes that are developmental precursors to conventional forms of reading and writing.

Empirical Research: refers to scientifically based research that applies rigorous, systematic, and objective procedures to obtain valid knowledge. This includes research that: employs systematic, empirical methods that draw on observation or experiment; has been accepted by a peer-reviewed journal or approved by a panel of independent experts through a comparably rigorous, objective, and scientific review; involves rigorous data analyses that are adequate to test the stated hypotheses and justify the general conclusions drawn; relies on measurements or observational methods that provide valid data across evaluators and observers and across multiple measurements and observations; and can be generalized.

English language learners: defined by the U.S. Department of Education as national-origin-minority students who are limited English proficient. Often abbreviated as ELLs.

Error correction: Immediate corrective feedback during reading instruction.

Etymology: the origin of a word and the historical development of its meaning (e.g., the origin of our word "etymology" comes from late Middle English: from Old French *ethimologie*, via Latin from Greek *etumologia*, from *etumologos*, "student of etymology," from *etumon*, neuter singular of *etumos* meaning "true").

Explicit instruction: instruction that involves direct explanation. The teacher's language is concise, specific, and related to the objective. Another characteristic of explicit instruction is a visible instructional approach which includes a high level of teacher/student interaction. Explicit instruction means that the actions of the teacher are clear, unambiguous, direct, and visible. This makes it clear what the students are to do and learn. Nothing is left to guesswork.

Expository text: reports factual information (also referred to as informational text) and the relationships among ideas. Expository text tends to be more difficult for students than narrative text because of the density of long, difficult, and unknown words or word parts.

Expressive language: language that is spoken.

Fidelity of implementation: the degree to which instruction follows the intent and design of the program.

Figurative meanings: language that departs from its literal meaning (e.g., the snow sparkled like diamonds; that child is a handful).

Five components of reading: phonemic awareness, phonics, fluency, vocabulary, and comprehension.

Flexible grouping: grouping students according to shared instructional needs and abilities and regrouping as their instructional needs change. Group size and allocated instructional time may vary among groups.

Floss rule: words of one syllable, ending in f, l, or s after one vowel, usually end in ff, ll, or ss (sounds /f/, /l/, /s/).

Fluency: ability to read text quickly, accurately, and with proper expression. Provides a bridge between word recognition and comprehension.

Fluency probe: an assessment for measuring fluency, usually a timed oral reading passage at the student's instructional reading level.

Formal assessment: follows a prescribed format for administration and scoring. Scores obtained from formal tests are standardized, meaning that interpretation is based on norms from a comparative sample of children.

Frayer model: an adaptation of the concept map. The framework of the Frayer Model includes: the concept word, the definition, characteristics of the concept word, examples of the concept word, and nonexamples of the concept word. It is important to include both examples and nonexamples, so students are able to identify what the concept word is and what the concept word is not.

Frustrational reading level: the level at which a reader reads at less than 90% accuracy (i.e., no more than one error per 10 words read). Difficult text for the reader.

Generalization: the ability to use a learned skill in novel situations.

Grapheme: a letter or letter combination that spells a phoneme; can be one, two, three, or four letters in English (e.g., e, ei, igh, eigh).

Graphic organizers: a visual framework or structure for capturing the main points of what is being read, which may include concepts, ideas, events, vocabulary, or generalizations. Graphic organizers allow ideas in text and thinking processes to become external by showing the interrelatedness of ideas, thus facilitating understanding for the reader. Structure is determined by the structure of the kind of text being read.

Graphophonemic: the relationship between letters and phonemes.

Guided Oral Reading: instructional support including immediate corrective feedback as students read orally.

Guided Practice: students practice newly learned skills with the teacher providing prompts and feedback.

High-frequency irregular words: words in print containing letters that stray from the most common sound pronunciation because they do not follow common phonic patterns (e.g., were, was, laugh, been).

High-frequency words: a small group of words (300–500) that account for a large percentage of the words in print and can be regular or irregular words (i.e., Dolch or Fry). Often, they are referred to as "sight words" because automatic recognition of these words is required for fluent reading.

Homograph: words that are spelled the same but have different origins and meanings. They may or may not be pronounced the same (e.g., *can* as in a metal container vs. *can* as in able to).

Homonym: words that sound the same but are spelled differently (e.g., cents vs. sense, knight vs. night).

Homophone: words that may or may not be spelled alike but are pronounced the same. These words are of different origins and have different meanings (e.g., ate and eight; scale as in the covering of a fish and scale as in a device used to weigh things).

Idiom: a phrase or expression that differs from the literal meaning of the words; a regional or individual expression with a unique meaning (e.g., it's raining cats and dogs).

Immediate corrective feedback: when an error occurs, the teacher immediately attends to it by scaffolding instruction (i.e., gradual release of responsibility).

Immediate intensive intervention: Instruction that may include more time, more opportunities for student practice, more teacher feedback, smaller group size, and different materials. Implemented as soon as assessment indicates that students are not making adequate progress in reading.

Implicit instruction: the opposite of explicit instruction, students discover skills and concepts instead of being explicitly taught. For example, the teacher writes a list of words on the board that begin with the letter "m" (mud, milk, meal, and mattress) and asks the students how the words are similar. The teacher elicits from the students that the letter "m" stands for the sound you hear at the beginning of the words.

Important words: unknown words that are critical to passage understanding and which students are likely to encounter in the future.

Independent reading level: the level at which a reader can read text with 95% accuracy (i.e., no more than one error per 20 words read). Relatively easy text for the reader.

Independent-instructional reading level range: the reading range that spans instructional and independent reading levels or level of text that a student can read with 90% to 95% or above accuracy.

Indirect vocabulary instruction: words learned through independent reading and conversation.

Inflectional suffix: in English, a suffix that expresses plurality or possession when added to a noun, tense when added to a verb, and comparison when added to an adjective and some adverbs. A major difference between inflectional and derivational morphemes is that inflections added to verbs, nouns, or adjectives do not change the grammatical role or part of speech of the base words (e.g., -s, -es, -ing, -ed).

Informal assessment: does not follow prescribed rules for administration and scoring and has not undergone technical scrutiny for reliability and validity; e.g., teacher-made tests, end-of-unit tests, and running records.

Informational text: nonfiction books, also referred to as expository text, that contain facts and information.

Initial instruction: first line of defense to prevent reading failure for all students. Instruction is provided in the whole-group (class) and small-group (differentiated) setting. A core reading program is the instructional tool used for initial instruction in Florida's Reading First initiative.

Instructional design: the process of translating key learning objectives and goals into a delivery system to meet those goals. When we discuss the instructional design of a reading program, we are referring to the underlying framework of a reading program, the way the curriculum is constructed.

Instructional reading level: the level at which a reader can read text with 90% accuracy (i.e., no more than one error per 10 words read). Engages the student in challenging but manageable text.

Instructional routines: include the following sequence of steps: (1) explicit instruction; (2) modeling; (3) guided practice; (4) student practice, application, and feedback; and (5) generalization.

Intensity: focused instruction in which students are academically engaged with the content and the teacher and receive more opportunities to practice with immediate teacher feedback.

Intervention instruction: provided only to students who are lagging behind their classmates in the development of critical reading skills. This instruction will usually be guided by a specific intervention program that focuses on one or more of the key areas of reading development. This type of instruction is needed by only a relatively small minority of students in a class. In some cases, students in second and third grade may have lagged so far behind grade level development of reading skills that very little content from the grade level comprehensive core program is suitable for them. In these cases, students may need to receive instruction guided by a comprehensive intervention program that is specifically designed to meet their needs while at the same time accelerating their growth toward grade-level reading ability.

Intervention program: provides content for instruction that is intended for flexible use as part of differentiated instruction and/or more intensive instruction to meet student learning needs in one or more of the specific areas of reading (phonological awareness, phonics, fluency, vocabulary, and comprehension). Provides targeted, intensive intervention for small groups of struggling readers.

Invented spelling: an attempt to spell a word based on a student's knowledge of the spelling system and how it works (e.g., kt for cat).

Irregular words: words that contain letters that stray from the most common sound pronunciation; words that do not follow common phonic patterns (e.g., were, was, laugh, been).

K-W-L: a technique used most frequently with expository text to promote comprehension. It can be used as a type of graphic organizer in the form of a chart, and it consists of a three-step process: What I Know (accessing prior knowledge), What I Want to Know (setting a purpose for reading), and What I Learned (recalling what has been read).

Learning communities: a group in which educators commit to ongoing learning experiences with a deliberate intent to transform teaching and learning at their school or within their district.

Letter combinations: also referred to as digraphs, a group of consecutive letters that represents a particular sound(s) in the majority of words in which it appears (e.g., /ai/ in maid; /ch/ in chair; /ar/ in car; /kn/ in know; /ng/ in ring).

Letter-sound correspondence: the matching of an oral sound to its corresponding letter or group of letters.

Linked: a clear connection among the objectives of what is taught within and across reading components (e.g., students learn some common letter sounds during phonics instruction, then read words that use those same letter sounds to practice fluency and develop vocabulary).

Listening vocabulary: the words needed to understand what is heard.

Literal comprehension: understanding of the basic facts that the student has read.

Main idea: the central thought or message of a reading passage.

Metacognition: an awareness of one's own thinking processes and how they work. The process of consciously thinking about one's learning or reading while actually being engaged in learning or reading. Metacognitive strategies can be taught to students; good readers use metacognitive strategies to think about and have control over their reading.

Modeling: teacher overtly demonstrates a strategy, skill, or concept that students will be learning.

Morpheme: the smallest meaningful unit of language.

Morphemic analysis: an analysis of words formed by adding prefixes, suffixes, or other meaningful word units to a base word.

Most common letter sounds: the sound that is usually pronounced for the letter when it appears in a short word, e.g. /a/ in apple.

Multisyllabic words: words with more than one syllable. A systematic introduction of prefixes, suffixes, and multisyllabic words should occur throughout a reading program. The average number of syllables in the words students read should increase steadily throughout the grades.

Narrative text: a story about fictional or real events.

Objectives: measurable statements detailing the desired accomplishments of a program.

Oddities: vowels that are pronounced differently from the expected pronunciation (e.g., the "o" in old is pronounced /ō/ instead of the expected /o/.

Onset and rime: in a syllable, the onset is the initial consonant or consonants, and the rime is the vowel and any consonants that follow it (e.g., in the word sat, the onset is "s" and the rime is "at"; in the word flip, the onset is "fl" and the rime is "ip").

Oral language: spoken language; its five components are phonology, morphology, syntax, semantics, and pragmatics.

Orthographic units: the representation of the sounds of a language by written or printed symbols.

Orthography: a writing system for representing language.

Outcome assessment: an assessment given at the end of the year for two purposes. First, they can help the principal and teachers in a school evaluate the overall effectiveness of their reading program for all students. Second, they are required in Reading First schools to help districts evaluate their progress toward meeting the goal of "every child reading on grade level" by third grade. Schools must show regular progress toward this goal to continue receiving Reading First funds.

Pacing: the pace of a lesson should move briskly, but not so fast as to rush students beyond their ability to answer correctly. The purposes for a fast pace are to help students pay close attention to the material being presented, and provide them with more practice time, which increases the opportunity for greater student achievement, keeps students actively engaged, and reduces behavior management problems by keeping students on task.

Partner/peer reading: students reading aloud with a partner, taking turns to provide word identification help and feedback.

Pedagogy: how instruction is carried out or the method and practice of teaching.

Phases of Word Learning:
  ➢ **Prealphabetic**—sight word learning at the earliest period. Children do not form letter-sound connections to read words; if they are able to read words at all, they do so by remembering selected visual features.
  ➢ **Partial alphabetic**—children learn the names or sounds of alphabet letters and use these to remember how to read words. However, they form connections between only some of the letters and sounds in words, often only the first and final letter-sounds.
  ➢ **Full alphabetic**—children can form complete connections between letters in written words and phonemes in pronunciations.
  ➢ **Consolidated alphabetic**—readers operate with multiletter units that may be morphemes, syllables, or subsyllabic units such as onsets and rimes. Common spelling patterns become consolidated into letter chunks, and these chunks make it easier to read words.

Phoneme: the smallest unit of sound within our language system. Combines with other phonemes to make words.

Phoneme isolation: recognizing individual sounds in a word (e.g., /p/ is the first sound in pan).

Phoneme manipulation: adding, deleting, and substituting sounds in words (e.g., add /b/ to oat to make boat; delete /p/ in pat to make at; substitute /o/ for /a/ in pat to make pot).

Phonemic awareness: the ability to notice, think about, or manipulate the individual phonemes in words; the understanding that sounds in spoken language work together to make words.

Phonic analysis: attention to various phonetic elements of words.

Phonics: the study of the relationships between letters and the sounds they represent; also used to describe reading instruction that teaches sound-symbol correspondences.

Phonogram: A succession of letters that represent the same phonological unit in different words, such as igh in flight, might, tight, sigh, and high.

Phonological awareness: One's sensitivity to, or explicit awareness of, the phonological structure of words in one's language. This is an "umbrella" term that is used to refer to a student's sensitivity to any aspect of phonological structure in language. Encompasses awareness of individual words in sentences, syllables, and onset-rime segments, as well as awareness of individual phonemes.

Prefix: a morpheme that precedes a root and that contributes to or modifies the meaning of a word (e.g., re in reprint).

Prior knowledge: Refers to schema, the knowledge and experience that readers bring to the text.

Progress monitoring: tests that keep the teacher informed about the child's progress in learning to read during the school year. These assessment results provide a quick sample of critical reading skills that will inform the teacher if the child is making adequate progress toward grade level reading ability at the end of the year.

Pronunciation guide: A key or guide consisting of graphic symbols that represent particular speech sounds.

Prosody: reading with expression, proper intonation, and phrasing. This helps readers to sound as if they are speaking the part they are reading. It is also this element of fluency that sets it apart from automaticity.

Rate: the speed at which a person reads.

Readability level: refers to independent, instructional, and frustrational levels of text reading.

Reading centers: special places organized in the classroom for students to work in small groups or pairs, either cooperatively or individually. Students work in centers while the teacher is conducting small group reading instruction. Each center contains meaningful, purposeful activities that are an extension and reinforcement of what has already been taught by the teacher in reading groups or in a large group. Reading centers offer students the opportunity to stay academically engaged as they apply the skills they have been learning. They are an excellent way for teachers to determine whether or not students know what they have been taught. It is important to develop a system and organize your classroom in such a way that you can provide feedback to students in a timely manner. Waiting until the end of the week to look at what students have worked on all week is not a productive use of instructional time, as students may have been practicing errors all week.

Examples of reading centers: Students practice phonics skills at the phonics center, sort word cards at the vocabulary center, and at the reading center, they read books, listen to taped books, record the reading of a book, and read in pairs. The reading center would contain a variety of books at various reading levels to meet the needs of all students. Other centers may consist of writing and spelling activities, pocket charts, white boards, magnetic letters to practice word building, sentence strips and word cards to create stories, sequencing activities with pictures, story boards, or sentence strips to retell a story that has been read. Some centers may be permanent; others will change according to the skills, books, and activities being currently addressed. It is recommended that teachers not bring in material from other content areas unless the activity from science or math, for example, specifically focuses on a skill that is being addressed in reading instruction. Reading centers require careful planning.

Reading fluency prorating formula: when students are asked to read connected text for more than one minute or less than one minute, their performance must be prorated to give a fluency rate per minute.

The prorating formula for this is the following: words read correctly x 60 ÷ by the number of seconds = Reading Fluency Score.

Reading vocabulary: The words needed to understand what is read.

Receptive language: language that is heard.

Regular words: any word in which each letter represents its respective, most common sound (e.g., sat, fantastic).

Repeated reading: rereading of text until the reader is able to read at a predetermined rate to produce fluency.

Retelling: recalling the content of what was read or heard.

Rhyming: words that have the same ending sound.

Root: a bound morpheme, usually of Latin origin, that cannot stand alone but is used to form a family of words with related meanings.

Scaffolding: refers to the support that is given to students in order for them to arrive at the correct answer. This support may occur as immediate, specific feedback that a teacher offers during student practice. For instance, the assistance the teacher offers may include giving encouragement or cues, breaking the problem down into smaller steps, using a graphic organizer, or providing an example. Scaffolding may be embedded in the features of the instructional design such as starting with simpler skills and building progressively to more difficult skills. Providing the student temporary instructional support assists them in achieving what they could not otherwise have done alone.

Schema: refers to prior knowledge, the knowledge and experience that readers bring to the text.

Schwa: the vowel sound sometimes heard in an unstressed syllable and is most often sounded as /uh/ or as the short /u/ sound as in cup.

Scientifically based reading research (SBRR): empirical research that applies rigorous, systematic, and objective procedures to obtain valid knowledge. This includes research that: employs systematic, empirical methods that draw on observation or experiment; has been accepted by a peer-reviewed journal or approved by a panel of independent experts through a comparably rigorous, objective, and scientific review; involves rigorous data analyses that are adequate to test the stated hypotheses and justify the general conclusions drawn; relies on measurements or observational methods that provide valid data across evaluators and observers and across multiple measurements and observations; and can be generalized.

Scope and sequence: a "road map" or "blueprint" for teachers that provides an overall picture of an instructional program and includes the range of teaching content and the order or sequence in which it is taught.

Screening: an informal inventory that provides the teacher a beginning indication of the student's preparation for grade level reading instruction; the "first alert" that a child may need extra help to make adequate progress in reading during the year.

Segmenting: separating the individual phonemes of a word into discrete units.

Self-monitoring: refers to metacognition. When students use self-monitoring strategies, they actively think about how they are learning or understanding the material, activities, or reading in which they are engaged.

Semantic feature analysis: uses a grid to help explore how a set of things are related to one another. By analyzing the grid one can see connections, make predictions, and master important concepts.

Semantic maps: portray the schematic relations that compose a concept; a strategy for graphically representing concepts.

Sight words: these are words that are recognized immediately. Sometimes sight words are thought to be irregular, or high-frequency words (e.g., the Dolch and Fry lists). However, any word that is recognized automatically is a sight word. May be phonetically regular or irregular.

Sound to symbol: phonics instruction that matches phoneme to grapheme.

Speaking vocabulary: the words used when speaking.

Speed: the rate at which a student reads.

Spelling patterns: refers to digraphs, vowel pairs, word families, and vowel variant spellings.

Stop sounds: a stop sound can only be said for an instant, otherwise its sound will be distorted (i.e., / b/, /c/ /d/, /g/, /h/, /j/, /k/, /p/, /q/, /t/, /x/). Words beginning with stop sounds are more difficult for students to sound out than words beginning with a continuous sound.

Story elements: characters, problem, solutions, themes, settings, and plot.

Story grammar: the general structure of stories that includes story elements.

Story maps: a strategy used to unlock the plot and important elements of a story. These elements can be represented visually through various graphic organizers showing the beginning, middle, and end of a story. Answering the questions of who, where, when, what, and how or why, and listing the main events is also part of story mapping. Also referred to as story grammar.

Strategic learners: active learners. While reading, these learners make predictions, organize information, and interact with the text. They think about what they are reading in terms of what they already know. They monitor their comprehension by employing strategies that facilitate their understanding.

Structural analysis: a procedure for teaching students to read words formed with prefixes, suffixes, or other meaningful word parts.

Student-friendly explanation: an explanation of the word's meaning rather than a definition, having the following traits: (1) characterizes the word and how it is typically used; and (2) explains the meaning in everyday language.

Suffix: an affix attached to the end of a base, root, or stem that changes the meaning or grammatical function of the word, as en in oxen.

Summarizing: reducing large selections of text to their bare essentials: the gist, the key ideas, the main points that are worth noting and remembering.

Supplemental instruction: instruction that goes beyond that provided by the comprehensive core program because the core program does not provide enough instruction or practice in a key area to meet the needs of the students in a particular classroom or school. For example, teachers in a school may observe that their comprehensive core program does not provide enough instruction in vocabulary, or in phonics, to adequately meet the needs of the majority of their students. They could then select a supplemental program in these areas to strengthen the initial instruction and practice provided to all students.

Syllable: a segment of a word that contains one vowel sound. The vowel may or may not be preceded and/or followed by a consonant.

Syllable types: there are six: (1) closed: cat, cobweb; (2) open: he, silo; (3) vowel-consonant-e (VCE): like, milestone; (4) consonant-l-e: candle, juggle (second syllable); (5) R-controlled: star, corner; and (6) vowel pairs: count, rainbow.

Symbol to sound: matching grapheme to phoneme.

Synonym: words that have similar meanings.

Systematic instruction: a carefully planned sequence for instruction, similar to a builder's blueprint for a house. A blueprint is carefully thought out and designed before building materials are gathered and construction begins. The plan for instruction that is systematic is carefully thought out, strategic, and designed before activities and lessons are planned. Instruction is across the five components (phonemic awareness, phonics, fluency, vocabulary, and comprehension). For systematic instruction, lessons build on previously taught information, from simple to complex.

Systematic phonics instruction: teaches children an extensive, prespecified set of letter-sound correspondences or phonograms.

Systematic review: a planned review of previously learned materials.

Targeted supplemental/intervention reading programs (TSRP/TIRP): these provide instruction in one or more areas of reading skill. They are intended for flexible use as part of differentiated instruction or in more intensive interventions to meet student learning needs in specific areas (phonemic awareness, phonics, fluency, vocabulary, or comprehension). When they are used with almost all students in the class because the CCRP does not provide enough instruction and practice in a given area for the majority of students in the class, they are usually referred to as supplemental materials. When they are used to provide targeted, intensive interventions for smaller groups of struggling readers, they are often referred to as intervention materials. Whether referred to as supplemental or intervention materials, these programs provide targeted instruction designed to fill in gaps in student knowledge or skill. These materials can be used to provide either additional instruction or additional practice, or both.

Target words: words specifically addressed, analyzed, and/or studied in curriculum lessons, exercises, and independent activities.

Text structure: the various patterns of ideas that are embedded in the organization of text (e.g., cause-effect, comparison-contrast, story grammar).

Think-alouds: during shared read aloud, teachers reveal their thinking processes by verbalizing: connections, questions, inferences, and predictions.

Timed reading: student reads appropriate text with a predetermined number of words to be read within a specific amount of time.

Trade book: A book intended for general reading that is not a textbook.

Train-the-trainer model: a capacity-building plan to develop master trainers who then deliver the program information to users.

Useful words: words that might be unknown to the student, but critical to passage understanding and words that students are likely to encounter in the future.

Useful letter sounds: letters that appear frequently in words. Beginning readers can decode more words when they know several useful letters. Knowing the sounds of /m/, /a/, /t/, and /i/ is more advantageous than the sounds /x/, /q/ /y/, and /z/. Other useful letter sounds are /a/, /e/, /i/, /o/, /u/, /b/, /c/, /d/, /f/, /g/, /h/, /k/, /l/, /n/, /p/, and /r/.

Variant correspondences: various corresponding spelling patterns for a specific sound or a variety of spelling patterns for one sound (e.g., long a spelled a, a_e, ai_, _ay).

Vocabulary: all of the words of our language. One must know words to communicate effectively. Vocabulary is important to reading comprehension because readers cannot understand what they are reading without knowing what most of the words mean. Vocabulary development refers to stored information about the meanings and pronunciation of words necessary for communication. Four types of vocabulary include listening, speaking, reading, and writing.

Vowel digraph or vowel pair: two vowels together that represent one phoneme, or sound (e.g., ea, ai, oa).

Word family: group of words that share a rime (a vowel plus the consonants that follow; e.g., -ame, -ick,-out).

Word learning strategies: strategies students use to learn words such as: decoding, analyzing meaningful parts of words, using analogy, using context clues, using a dictionary (student friendly definitions), glossary, or other resources.

Word parts: letters, onsets, rimes, syllables that, when combined, result in words. The ability to recognize various word parts in multisyllabic words is beneficial in decoding unfamiliar words.

Word study: the act of deliberately investigating words (e.g., vocabulary-building exercises, word-identification practice, and spelling).

Writing vocabulary: words that a student might use while writing.

About the Authors

Ellen Burns Hurst, a native of Atlanta, GA, holds a Ph.D. in language and literacy. A true pioneer in the field of dyslexia, her passion for working with struggling readers is exemplified by her work as an intervention/reading specialist for 35 years in the public and private sectors. At the heart of this passion is the desire to level the achievement playing field for all children. Dr. Hurst continues to focus on changing the reading lives of students through her private practice and research presentations at national and international literacy conferences.

Michael Richard Hurst, J.D., has been a practicing attorney in Atlanta for 35 years. He is currently specializing in educational advocacy.